# Making Love

## How to Create, Enjoy, and Sustain Intimacy

### Dr. Robert Johansen

### and

### Dr. Todd Gaffaney

*Making Love: How to Create, Enjoy and Sustain Intimacy*
By Dr. Robert Johansen and Dr. Todd Gaffaney

Copyright 2017 by Dr. Robert Johansen and Dr. Todd Gaffaney
Cover Copyright 2017 by Untreed Reads Publishing
Cover Design by Ginny Glass

ISBN-13: 978-1-94544-752-5

Also available in ebook format.
Previously published in print, 2010

Published by Untreed Reads, LLC
506 Kansas Street, San Francisco, CA 94107
www.untreedreads.com

Printed in the United States of America.

**Publisher's Note**

# Acknowledgments

To my wife, Anne, thank you for being the loving catalyst to the ideas contained in this book. Words fall short of capturing my gratitude for your unwavering support and devotion. Todd and I will always be grateful for your practical suggestions.

To my son, Dr. Ian Johansen, thank you for your love, support, and prodding. Your labors gave the armchair theorizing of our intimacy model a scientific footing. Todd and I will always be grateful to you.

To my daughter, Lauren, thank you for your love, inspiration, and encouragement.

To my parents, Nils and Naomi, your love was formative.

— *Robert Johansen*

To my wife, Vi, and our family, Mat, Wendy, and Sherice, thank you for the opportunity to know myself better. I appreciate all of your loving support and ideas. It has been a long haul. Vi, you even had the time to remodel the house.

To Bob, thank you for your wise and clever feedback. Your humorous margin notes took the edge off.

To John, thank you for having confidence in our project.

Lastly, our thanks to the many clients who supported and inspired us.

— *Todd Gaffaney*

i

# Contents

# Introduction

*Making Love* is not an instructional manual on human sexuality. It is instead a recipe for how couples can create, enjoy, and sustain intimacy.

## The Revealed Relationship

Intimacy is the most powerful and unique relationship we will ever experience. The magic of intimacy is its power to reveal who we are—all of our flaws, foibles, and imperfections are drawn into the open. Nobody knows us better than our intimate partners. They provoke us to experience the parts of our personalities that are not fully developed. Now here's the dilemma—what do we do? On the one hand, we can get defensive, withdraw, or argue. Intimacy suffers. On the other hand, intimacy makes possible our fullest maturity as a person. It is the new womb of development.

## Two Kinds of Love

Do you remember the first time you fell in love? How did you explain your passionate feelings? Typically, we attribute our attraction to the traits found in our romantic partners. "He's so intelligent." "She's so sexy." We fall in love with who we perceive them to be. In this book, we refer to this as *character-based love*.

Character-based love places the source of our love within our partners. Our love then becomes too dependent on our partners, and we lose control of our affections. Worse, when our partners' traits change or disappear—and they will—what happens to our love? Character-based love is seriously flawed.

Alternatively, *self-generated love* presupposes that what we feel for our partners ought to be our own creation. It should not depend solely on the traits in our partners. Love develops from the kind of people we are when we are with our partners. If I like who I am when I'm with you, then I like you too.

1

The centerpiece of self-generated love is effective need management. Our focus should not be on need gratification or on partner compatibility (many self-help books stress these ideas). The key is to create and maintain respect for who I am in relation to you. This requires careful and well-practiced need management. I must identify, legitimatize, and represent the needs I bring to my relationship. This is the way I grow love for myself and my partner. I am self-generating love.

If you need help applying the concepts in the book or would like us to present the model to you or your group, please contact us at 714-651-8853, or email us at rjohansenphd@verizon.net or tgaffaney@cerritos.edu.

# Part I
# Problems and Solutions

# Chapter One
# Why Relationships Fail

Relationships fail. Intimacy is difficult. Oddly enough, it's easier to cure most forms of cancer than it is to heal a dying relationship. The divorce rate for couples married after 1990 is a staggering 67%! Even marriage counselors divorce at or around the national average. While these statistics are sobering, there is hope.

## Character-Based Love

Our relationships fail because the love we have for our partners is *character-based.* Simply put, character-based love is the attraction we feel for another person based upon his or her personality traits. This is the usual way we fall in love. Not surprisingly, character-based love is most prominent throughout the dating process when we least know our partners. During this romantic phase, we are passionate about our partners because of the type of people we perceive them to be. We idealize them. They are "kind," "intelligent," "physically attractive," "fun to be with," and so on. We love them because they possess these traits. The belief is that these character traits are sufficient to create and maintain our affections over a lifetime.

We explain the love we feel for our partners as the direct consequence of their character traits. Character-based love places the source of our love outside ourselves, and so we lose control of our affections. Without our being fully aware of it, the source of our feelings is turned over to our partners, making them responsible for the creation and maintenance of our affections. This very common mentality unfortunately forecasts the erosion of intimacy.

It is important to note that, when we place the source of our love outside of ourselves, it prevents us from looking inward and

5

developing the kind of skills we need for intimacy. To make matters worse, when we ascribe positive traits to our partners, we simultaneously but unwittingly make them responsible for gratifying our needs. We reinforce our belief that they are the primary source of our love. However, when they fail to meet our needs—and they will—we blame them for not caring. We accuse them of having changed. In this sense, character-based love is the wellspring of poor personal need management.

Take a moment and reflect on the idea of character-based love. Ask yourself, what attracted you to your partner? What traits did you admire? Did these same traits form the basis of your love? If so, has your perception of these traits changed?

### A Case Example

Jeff and Heather fell madly in love with each other. Jeff couldn't take his eyes off of Heather's voluptuous body. Sealing the deal, Heather was financially well-off and had an engaging personality and an infectious laugh. Since Jeff came from humble beginnings, he was insecure about money. Heather seemed to be just the solution he needed. She was the perfect match. Now, here it comes: Jeff s love of Heather is character-based.

The greatest pitfall of character-based love is that we project the source of our love onto another person. We externalize the origin of our affections. In effect, our love is dependent upon how we perceive our partners. If they change—and they do—what happens to our love?

Here's another example. When Maria first met Reuben, she described him to her friends as "confident," "positive," and a "take-charge kind of guy." She was drawn to these traits. Now, let's jump ahead in time five years. Maria and Reuben are having marital problems. Maria now describes Reuben as "dominating and controlling." Why did her initial attraction reverse itself? Did Reuben change, or did Maria's perception of Reuben's traits change? Either way, the source of her love was external and not under her own control. It was character-based. Maria and Reuben are in trouble; their relationship is at risk.

Maria and Reuben are a typical couple. The way they met and the problems that surfaced between them represent the norm and not the exception. Maria and Reuben fell in love the same way that most of us do. They found traits in each other they liked and presumed they were reasonably and sufficiently compatible. Unfortunately, their character-based love is at best incomplete. At worst, it spells disaster. At this point, let's deepen our analysis of character-based love and its role in the demise of our relationships.

## Four Pathways

Character-based love encompasses *four major pathways* leading to relationship failure. Each of these pathways explains in its own way why intimate relationships are difficult and often fail.

First, *romance is never enough; it is the quintessential form of character-based love.* The initial passionate forces of attraction are important, but not sufficient to sustain us through the rigors of an intimate relationship. Romance has us fall in love with the traits in our partner. While this is commonplace, the danger is that the source of our love lies outside ourselves. It's not under our control. This type of love assumes that our partners will never change, or that our perceptions of them will never change.

Second, *we suffer from low intimacy intelligence.* Character-based love seduces us into concluding that the reason for our love lies in the traits of our partner. Because of this belief, we fail to develop the real intimacy skills necessary to navigate and sustain a long-term relationship. Without these internal skills, the difficulties of intimacy can be overwhelming.

Third, *we fail to overcome childhood emotional wounds.* These early emotional injuries, whether slight or severe, divert emotional development and ultimately jeopardize our current intimate relationships. To compensate, we often seek and become attracted to traits in our partners that we think will make up for the deficiencies in ourselves. We make our partners what we need them to be in an effort to make ourselves more complete, more whole. This is another negative of character-based love.

Fourth, *gender differences ignite conflict.* The differences between men and women both attract and repel us. They set the stage for the longest war. We place our partners into sex roles that are character-based. We then relate to our partners on the basis of these characterizations and often fail to see exceptions in their behavior. Stereotypically, men are expected to be strong and women are expected to be nurturing. When our partners fall short of these social expectations, problems often arise.

The four pathways of character-based love explain why intimate relationships fail. Because each of these potentially venomous pathways extends deeply into our relationships, we are going to examine them in greater detail and preview what can be done about them.

## Romance Is Never Enough

Of the many reasons for commitment and marriage, romance generally tops the list and stands out as the most compelling. Romance is captivating! It affirms our worth, fills our emptiness, and celebrates our individual sense of purpose and meaning. It's no wonder we attempt to keep it permanent through the commitment of marriage. If it were not for the powerful feelings of romance, we might never take on the sacrifices, self-denial, difficult compromises, and troublesome conflicts that are a part of every marriage.

Yet for all that romance seems to promise, it is a potential minefield. An ancient proverb reads *amanitas amenities,* meaning "Lovers are mad." In 1949, a European social critic by the name of Denis de Rougemont stated that we are in the midst of a most pathological experiment, namely, basing marriage that is lasting upon romance, which is a passing passion. The logical outcome of marriage based solely on romance is divorce. Marriage can kill romance. Romance suggests unending perfect love, passion, and excitement. In reality, marriage means responsibility, imperfect love, and risky self-exposure.

It is chancy to begin marriage solely on romance. Romance blinds us to the fact that marriage is unique and stands apart from all other relationships. It is the most complex and difficult partnership. Successful marriage is a disciplined art; it requires self-knowledge and self-management. Romance, on the other hand, can be whimsical and carefree—or it can be reckless and destructive.

In short, romance should be viewed as a starting point. It must be welcomed as a good but incomplete tool at the start of a long project that will require using a number of additional tools in order to be successful.

Obviously, we need more than romance to maintain a long-term intimate relationship. In the final analysis, for all its intoxicating joys, romance is character-based. Remember, when we are attracted to our partners' qualities, we unknowingly place the source of our love outside ourselves. We then become dependent on our partners for the creation, maintenance, and quality of our feelings. Our love is partner-directed.

Character-based love is ultimately flawed. What happens when our partners' traits change, or our perception of these same qualities shifts? When these inevitable changes occur, they rock the foundation of a couple's love. When a partner's traits change or even disappear, so do the positive feelings. Love is on borrowed time. It will atrophy and die.

But there's another option: *We keep the source of our feelings within ourselves. Love is to be self-generated and under our control. By this means, we create and maintain love for our partner.* This point will be elaborated in Chapter Two.

## Low Intimacy Intelligence

The second reason relationships fail is that people lack intimacy skills. This failure is the direct by-product of character-based love. By focusing on our partners' character traits, our attention is turned away from developing our own internal intimacy skills. The hidden assumption is that love is something that *happens* to us as opposed to something we create on our own. With this in mind, let's define and explore the specific skills of intimacy. Before we talk about intimacy, however, consider a few pertinent questions about your *intimacy intelligence.*

How much of your love for your partner is character-based? Are you fully intimate with your partner? Would your partner agree? Go ahead and ask him or her! Now consider this point. Have you ever thought you could improve the quality of intimacy with practice?

### Intimacy Defined

Intimacy is the degree of emotional closeness between two people. It requires time to develop. There is a slow accumulation of shared experience that can only take place over time. There are no shortcuts. Short-term relationships are simply not as intimate as long-term relationships.

Intimacy requires a range of relating. It is not only important to know a person over time. One must know one's partner in a variety of settings, such as work, school, play, and family. For example, you might find yourself attracted to someone at a party, but when you see the person at his or her workplace, you may be disappointed.

Further, intimacy involves opening up to our partners. We need to disclose to our partners important information about ourselves (needs and feelings). A renowned Yale psychologist, Sid Jourard, said, "Self-disclosure begets self-disclosure." When we open up, the chances are high our partners will open up too. Intimacy deepens.

Lastly, intimacy implies a tolerance for closeness with others. The ability to get close and sustain closeness is different for each person. Early relationship experience of closeness obviously will lay a firm foundation for future trusting relationships. Now: What is your tolerance for intimacy? We are going to test you later.

### The Intricacies of Intimacy

Intimacy is difficult. It requires contrary behaviors: discipline and practice and also a revealing of our vulnerabilities. It can elude even our best efforts. There are no formal institutions that prepare us for the demands of intimacy. For most of us, it is a matter of trial and error, or learn as you go. Intimacy requires more from us than simply sharing our feelings. It engages our whole personality. We must be brave and trusting.

For real intimacy, trust is a two-way street. Beliefs about our partners and ourselves are in free flow, spontaneous, kind, and considerate. We expect our partners to be predictable and dependable. We adjust our closeness to our partners based upon our immediate experiences and our knowledge of our shared history. If our partners meet our expectations, then we are likely to trust them. We believe our partners are safe, and intimacy moves forward.

Intimacy also requires self-trust. This demands knowledge, acceptance, and expression of our needs and expectations. The capacity for self-trust makes it possible for us to confidently move ahead into the world of relationships. When we are confident in ourselves, our partners do not have to be perfect. Other people can let us down, but we retain the ability to adjust and secure our needs. For instance, Sean's frustration over his wife's lack of enthusiasm for tennis didn't deter him from going ahead with his own plans to learn the game. While understanding her reluctance, he still had the capacity to trust his judgment and make decisions that were best for him.

11

And intimacy is courage. It takes courage to get close to someone. The danger is that we can get embarrassed, rejected, or otherwise hurt. There is no guarantee of safety in intimacy. It is like going into the lion's den. It takes courage to consciously reveal our deepest needs and the feelings associated with them. Whether we consciously choose to open up or not, intimacy will inevitably reveal our strengths and weaknesses in one form or another. There are no exceptions. None of us is exempt. Intimacy ultimately requires courage to assume responsibility for what gets revealed.

Intimacy reveals. It spotlights how well we manage our needs. Fear of embarrassment and rejection must be overcome. And failure to manage our needs can spell disaster. But the courage required for good need management builds love for ourselves and our partners. It also overcomes the limitations of character-based love.

Intimacy is a paradox. We need to have close relationships, yet at the same time we need to be separate individuals. The paradox here is that we cannot experience our full separateness unless we have close attachments. The reverse is also true. We cannot be fully attached until we experience our full separateness. John Bowlby, a noted authority on relationships, said, "We are our happiest when our lives are organized around a series of excursions, both short and long, from our secured attachments." Intimacy delicately balances our attachment to others against our capacity for separateness and individuality.

Many people fail the challenges of intimacy. As we've mentioned, people often lack the skills to develop and maintain a close relationship. Again, how would you evaluate your own intimacy skills? If you have the courage, and we're betting you do, take the Intimacy Questionnaire.

## The Intimacy Questionnaire

We have devised a method of evaluating what we call *intimacy intelligence.* Qualities such as self-knowledge, self-expressiveness, being close while preserving one's independence, the capacity to take on another's perspective, the ability to regulate emotions and resolve conflict, are all necessary for the development of a close and lasting partnership.

Now, test yourself to assess your current level of intimacy intelligence. Rate yourself in the following categories on each of the statements by selecting the number that best fits. Take your time and really think about yourself and your relationship.

### INTIMACY INTELLIGENCE QUESTIONNAIRE

Use the rating scale below to evaluate your intimacy skills.

**Never (0) Rarely (1) Sometimes (2) Usually (3) Always (4)**

### Self-knowledge

___ 1. I know why I behave the way I do in my relationship.

___ 2. I am aware of my needs in my relationship.

___ 3. I am aware of the feelings my partner elicits in me.

___ 4. I am aware of my strengths and weaknesses.

___ 5. I know what makes me happy and what makes me sad.

### Self-Expressiveness

___ 1. I can assert my feelings and needs in my relationship.

___ 2. I can ask for what I want in my relationship.

___ 3. I can say no without feeling guilty.

___ 4. I can set limits in my relationships.

___ 5. I can give and receive negative feedback with my partner.

### Dependence/Independence

___ 1. I can depend on my partner to meet my needs.

___ 2. I can make my own decisions.

___ 3. I can be close and still maintain my independence.

___ 4. I can act freely and comfortably in the absence of my partner.

___ 5. I can ask for affection and support from my partner.

### Empathy

___ 1. I can understand my partner's emotions.

___ 2. I know how my partner thinks under many circumstances.

___ 3. I can switch my perspective to my partner's with ease.

___ 4. I know my partner's likes and dislikes.

___ 5. I know my partner's sensitive points.

### Conflict Management

___ 1. I am good at resolving conflicts with my partner.

___ 2. I would rather solve problems than win an argument.

___ 3. I am open to my partner's proposed solutions.

___ 4. I can see both sides of a conflict.

___ 5. I can solve problems without becoming defensive.

### Intimacy Tolerance

___ 1. I am at ease when my partner expresses deep feelings.

___ 2. I would like to be closer to my partner.

___ 3. I enjoy getting close to others.

___ 4. The closer I am to my partner, the better I feel.

___ 5. I can talk openly about my commitment to my partner.

Add your ratings to create a total score, which will give you a reasonable estimate of your current level of intimacy with your partner. The higher your score, the easier it will be to implement the new concepts presented in this book. If your scores are low, your chances of a failed relationship go up proportionately. So, if your score is in the 90 to 150 range, your intimacy level is on the high side. On the other hand, if your score is less than 30, your intimacy level is on the low side. Scores between 30 and 90 are considered in the average range.

Don't be too critical of yourself if you didn't score in the range you would like. (One of the authors was surprised about his own low score on self-assertion.) Since most of us have no formal training in intimacy, we will present a model in Chapter Two that should increase your scores considerably and improve your current relationship.

The upside to intimacy is that anyone can learn this skill. With time, practice, and a change in how you look at love, you can improve your intimacy skills. In the next chapter we will present a model on how to develop intimacy skills, and we will discuss how these skills can be used to bring positive change to our relationships.

## The Incompleteness of Childhood

The argument just got hotter. She yelled. He yelled back louder. It almost came to blows. Her tears flowed. He ran out.

Sound familiar? Have you been in arguments like this that left you feeling totally unloved, hurt, and angry? Have you said or done something damaging to your partner and later regretted it? All of us have at one time or another reacted in an explosive, crazy, or illogical fashion and later wondered why. Many of these intense reactions have their origins in our past relationships. Early negative relationship experience shapes the structure of our brains, setting us up for relationship failure.

## The Two Brains

Every brain is unique. Our brains are different because of our genes and our experiences. Genes do not act alone in shaping our brains. Nobel prize–winning psychiatrist Eric Kandel, M.D., stated, "Gene expression is a function of learning and experience." In other words, brain development depends on our experience. Early relationship experiences play the heaviest role in our emotional development. And these early experiences always impact our current intimate relationships. Let's see how this can happen.

Each of us has an emotional and a rational brain. The emotional brain is involved in our survival. It regulates basic life functions such as hunger, thirst, and metabolism. In addition, it organizes the emotional experiences connected to our earliest and most critical relationships. Early stable and nurturing relationships create ideal circumstances for brain development.

Unfortunately, the opposite is also true: early relationship crises and abuse lay down nerve tracts in our brains that can make future relationships very difficult. The emotional brain can actually monopolize our brain's resources, especially during times of relationship crisis. During times of intense emotion, our rational brain centers are actually bypassed, setting us up for strong emotional and physical reactions. This is why our emotions sometimes prevail over reasoning and better judgment.

The emotional brain is largely in control during early childhood, recording and storing significant relationship experiences. These early interactions with our caretakers establish deep neural and hormonal pathways which literally shape the architecture of our brain.

Specifically, when we have been hurt and it has not been adequately resolved, these neural pathways make us acutely sensitive to similar types of negative experiences. The emotional brain then prevents us from creating adaptive and rational responses. In other words, we bring a child-like reactivity to events that require adult-like responses. The bottom line is that our emotional brain naturally takes a firm hold of negative experiences and stubbornly won't allow us to forget them.

The rational brain, on the other hand, is composed of higher brain centers that control thinking, judging, and reasoning. This part of our brain is slow in developing and adapts to situations based on logic and reason. But because of the rational brain's late emergence on the developmental scene, the emotional brain retains greater control over our reactions to our relationships. This is plainly seen in our knee-jerk reactions to our mates when we have been hurt.

However, when we *resolve* traumatic experiences, we transfer the painful emotional memories to higher brain centers. Here, they are organized in new ways that allow us to have greater control and a broader range of choices.

These points are somewhat technical and dry, but we thought it might be helpful for you to understand how the emotional brain works under crisis. Every one of us experiences emotional emergencies of some kind or another. These crises register deep within our emotional brains and become a force to be reckoned with, especially in our intimate relationships.

### The Ghosts of the Past

Early painful experiences haunt us. Shame, rejection, fighting, abuse, and loss are all stamped deeply into our brains. This is especially obvious in people who have suffered severe abuse as children. Left untreated, these overwhelming and unhealed emotional injuries severely impact our relationships.

Why does this happen? Emotional conflicts threaten us. Under crisis, our emotional brain is activated, hormones flow, blood pressure increases. Then our earliest and least developed strategies for protecting ourselves against hurt come back into play, most often in a disruptive manner.

Noted author Sam Keen wrote, "None of us escapes our childhood without suffering some degree of emotional hurt and trauma." These wounds leave scars. Here's a personal example. One of the authors was adopted at the age of four. The parental abandonment leading to his adoption left him feeling empty. This emptiness has challenged him considerably, especially when it comes to forming trusting relationships. His past definitely haunts him.

How do we make up for the deficiencies of our childhood? There are two ways. The easier way is to look to our partners to complete us, much like a child looks to a parent for emotional resources. We look for traits in our partners to remedy our shortcomings. While this is not uncommon, it is character-based, and as such is rife with the potential for relationship disaster.

The more difficult path is to repair our own deficiencies. In this way, we learn to become our own parent. We learn how to manage our needs instead of looking to our partners for the answers. This is a key point that we'll develop later in Chapter Two.

Our unresolved emotional reactions to past life events do not have to be extreme to have a negative impact on our lives. Even milder stressors involving everyday conflicts and common misunderstandings between people can leave their marks on our brains and interfere with our current and future relationships. Let's examine this point by looking at the example of Ken and Brittany.

Ken has an abusive habit of controlling Brittany. He makes all the important decisions in the family and discourages Brittany from working outside the home. How did Ken learn to relate to Brittany in this way? He learned to be controlling from his mother. Ken's mother was a single parent of four children, and in order to manage the household she ran roughshod over the entire family.

Ken grew up believing that mature adults should be in charge. Now, whenever Ken and Brittany are faced with making family decisions, Ken takes control, overreacting to Brittany's gentler style. This suggests that Ken's emotional brain has been activated and, like a false alarm, is alerting him to the potential dangers of Brittany's passive behaviors. He is not able to step back and rationally assess his situation.

The ghosts of Ken's past are alive and well. His past experiences with his mother dictate his current reactions to his wife. In fact, it's possible Ken may have chosen Brittany in large part because of her passive traits. By choosing a weak partner, Ken looks strong and in control. This is another manifestation of character-based love.

Are there any ghosts in your past? If so, how are they haunting you? Do you look to your partner to make up for your deficiencies? Later, we will discuss how you can overcome emotional wounds. We will show you a model that will help you resolve early relationship experience.

## The War of the Sexes

The war of the sexes is a war of misunderstandings. In Deborah Tannen's classic book on gender communications, *You Just Don't Understand*, she gives a simple but common example in which a wife tells her husband that she is thirsty. He responds by bringing her a glass of water. Unfortunately, and to his surprise, his gesture is met with a cool indifference. What happened?

This example illustrates a common gender miscommunication. The husband felt that his actions were both efficient and compassionate. Unfortunately, what his wife wanted him to do was to empathize with her feelings. Instead, he wanted to please her with a practical solution to her problem, while she simply wanted to share her feelings. He was hurt because she had rejected his gesture of love. She, in turn, was hurt because he had completely misconstrued her intentions.

Actually, neither one of them communicated in a language the other could understand. They were blinded by their gender roles.

His role was to solve the problem; hers was to connect. His masculine image left him thinking that he should rescue her. Her feminine image left her thinking that if he really loved her, he would know what she needed. In the end, both felt misunderstood and hurt. Each partner acted according to his or her gender role expectations, and this is yet another example of character-based love.

On the surface, the previous illustration may seem trivial. However, it is precisely these everyday types of problems that have the potential to get out of hand. Consider what happened to one of the authors:

"I had an argument with my wife over the whereabouts of a sleeping bag that we needed for our daughter's overnight party. I thought that the item had been lost, while she thought the sleeping bag had been lent to a friend. She wanted me to phone the friend to have it returned. I disagreed, insisting again that it was lost. Soon, she began to get impatient and angry, demanding that I call the friend.

"What I did at this point averted a major argument. I reluctantly gave in and made the call. To my surprise, our friend did have the sleeping bag. I had been wrong. I painfully acknowledged my mistake and apologized to my wife. The apology wasn't easy for me. Like most men, I am sensitive to any challenge to my position as strong, competent, and knowledgeable."

From the male perspective, apologies suggest weakness and self-doubt, two traits that stand at odds with ideal masculinity. Alternatively, the author's wife was equally challenged with conflicting feelings. She was absolutely sure of the whereabouts of the sleeping bag. Her anger conveyed how difficult it was to declare what she knew to be true without putting her relationship with her husband at risk.

## The Clashing of Values

In spite of the past one hundred years of feminist activism and the relatively recent efforts to raise male awareness, men and women perceive their gender roles differently. In other words, we continue to stereotype each other. Unfortunately, we continue to oversimplify traits about each gender. He assumes traits in her and she assumes traits in him. And this is especially true when it comes to the management of our emotions.

While gender stereotypes are common, actual researched-based gender differences are relatively few and small in scale. In fact, there are greater individual differences within each gender group than there are differences between gender groups. For example, there are men who stay at home to parent their children, single mothers who work two jobs while raising a family, and women executives who are career-oriented and choose not to be mothers.

When we stereotype each other, we act on the basis of our preconceived expectations, and in so doing, we experience a clashing of values. He values one thing, she values another. These differing expectations often create tension and conflict. Regardless of whether these gender differences are real or not, our differing expectations of each other create conflict, and these clashes need to be managed. This is where character-based love once again can be seen rearing its ugly head.

Gender differences exist, whether they are based in science or assumptions we make about each gender. The important point is that these differences or stereotypes must be managed. When we attribute gender traits to our partners (real or assumed), we again place the source of our control outside ourselves. We make our partner the alpha and omega of our affections. This is character-based love.

In broad-brushed, but valid terms, many men expect themselves to act strong and many women expect themselves to

21

act caring. These are potent character-based traits by which men and women not only define their worth, but fall in love with each other. Some women are attracted to men whom they perceive to be strong and competent. Some men are drawn to women whom they judge to be kind and nurturing.

This way of stereotyping is common, but it is nevertheless character-based loving. If her love of him is primarily based on her perception of him as strong, what happens when he is not? Likewise, what happens to his love for her when circumstances make it impossible for her to be caring? We expect the impossible from ourselves and our partners!

Further, men and women often have different gender values, and this can lead to serious character-based conflict. He may value career, money, status, and power, all of which create a sense of his strength. She, on the other hand, may organize her self-worth largely around the quality of her connections with family and friends. Of course, there are some men who stay at home as the primary caretakers of the children and many women who excel in the workplace and are the main breadwinners. Regardless of who stays home and who earns the money, there is the potential for a clashing of values.

### Male Stereotypes

Speaking in stereotypical terms, for a man to achieve success, as he defines it, he must bury his weak feelings in order to hold an image of himself as competent, strong, and independent. Of course, none of this prepares him for the demands of intimacy. Since he is largely unaware of his feelings, his ability to communicate intimately is severely hampered. In fact, he may appraise his worth in terms of his "strength" and by what he "provides" for his family instead of the quality of time he spends with them.

Sensing his lack of connectedness, his partner often feels angry and resentful. How she expresses her emotional needs for closeness is crucial. If she criticizes him for his independence and ambition, he will feel misunderstood. Ironically, he feels he is showing his love by playing strong and providing for his family. Further, he may feel hurt and confused because he is being attacked for the very traits he values most in himself.

### Female Stereotypes

In order for a woman to achieve success, as she defines it, she must feel connected to her partner, family, and friends. If this is missing, then she is at a loss. In this example, nothing compensates her in the same way as closeness to family and friends. Her feminine traits set the stage for two major conflicts. First, she may rely too heavily upon her partner for financial support. This can leave her feeling dependent. Second, her need for closeness can backfire on her. In her efforts to be close and her sacrifice for her loved ones, she may lose her identity.

His reactions to her dilemma also create a clash. He has mixed feelings about her dependency. On the one hand, her dependency complements and affirms his need to appear strong and in charge. On the other hand, he may lose respect for her due to her own lack of identity and strength.

When we pigeonhole our partners into rigid roles, we create character-based problems. At times, he may need her to act weak in order to feel strong. What is she to do? At other times, her weakness is a turn-off. What is he to do?

Do your values clash? Are there negative consequences? If you are a man, how do you define success? If you are a woman, how do you define success? Can you find character-based issues and gender-related problems in your relationship?

### Gender Fallout

Gender differences can lead to labeling or name-calling, another destructive form of character-based relating. For example, she describes him as selfish and uncaring—a real "jerk!" He describes her as too emotional and critical—a real "nag!"

Once labeled, we respond to our partners in terms of the label and ignore other aspects about them. For example, when he labels her a "nag," he reacts to her critical nature and fails to remember those times when she is kind, patient, and happy. When she labels him an "uncaring jerk," she may not see those times when he is sensitive, warm, or affectionate. In a real sense, the label obscures a more complete view of our partners.

Labeling also creates negative reactions. These include distancing and verbal attacks. For example, during a heated argument, a wife calls her husband a "jerk" (verbal attack). In response, he shuts down his feelings and wants to escape, probably by zoning out in front of the television (distancing).

After prolonged use, these types of reactions become automatic. He does not think. Instead, he simply reacts in the predictable way. As we have said, when he calls her a nag, or she calls him a jerk, powerful negative feelings are brought up. These negative feelings need to be managed effectively, or the possibility for constructive communication breaks down.

Gender fallout poses an enormous challenge. Our sex roles can be instances of character-based loving. By attributing gender traits to our partners, we expect them to behave in a certain way. When they don't, we are left with negative feelings. We've lost control of our affections.

But our gender differences don't have to spell disaster. Instead, our differences can create opportunities for self-growth and improvement in our relationships. We believe that gender differences can be complementary instead of antagonistic. For instance, she disciplines the children, he plays with them. Do they have to be at odds with each other, or can these differences be integrated to form a more complete union of opposites? In Chapter Six, we will suggest an alternative way of looking at gender conflicts and point out how to effectively manage these differences.

# Reflections and Questions

After reading this chapter, you may feel discouraged. How can you attain the impossible and build an intimate relationship? Don't most relationships fail? Actually, it is true that intimate relationships are difficult, and many of them do fail. But just because your relationship fails doesn't mean *you* are a failure.

How can we learn from our failed relationships? When studied, they become mentors for future relationships. Intimate relationships—successful or not—are precisely the kind of relationships that allow us the opportunity for self-examination and self-growth. Later, we'll show how this can be done.

# Personal Exercise

You can make this chapter more personally meaningful by reflecting on your own relationship. Suppose you find yourself with serious relationship problems and you're considering breaking up. Before you do anything, see if you can pinpoint the sources of your difficulties. In what way is your problem character-based?

1. Have your romantic feelings died?
2. Do you or your partner lack intimacy skills?
3. Do your current problems have a past history?
4. Do your problems stem from gender differences?

Remember, these are the four major problems of character-based love.

Your efforts to study the origins of your problems and the needs and feelings associated with them will pay off. Imagine suddenly finding blood oozing from a wound on your body. What would you do? Of course, you'd want to do more than just wipe away the blood. You'd want to know the exact nature of your wound so that you could apply the most appropriate treatment. The same applies to our emotional reactions to our partners. We need to study these reactions for what they can tell us about ourselves, our emotional maturity, and our relationships.

# Chapter Two
# A New Model for Lasting Relationships

An intimate relationship is like no other relationship. It lays open our inner selves like a surgeon's scalpel, revealing who we are. Intimacy ignites our most extreme, basic, and raw feelings of love and hate. Intimacy invites conflict. It frustrates and provokes us. It demands enormous time and energy. Intimacy is even frightening and painful, yet no other relationship promises us the same opportunity for personal gratification, growth, and fulfillment.

## Introduction to the Model

Stop for a moment and think about the last argument you had with your partner. There were no winners. Consider what really happened. You and your partner were defensive and blamed one another for not gratifying each other's needs. Without a doubt, blaming is the most common cover-up for what intimacy reveals about us. Intimacy reveals every flaw, foible, and imperfection in our characters. There is no escape. Being revealed for our weaknesses can provoke us to withdraw, or to blame and fight. Obviously, this is counterproductive.

Instead, we are going to teach you to use a new model. It stresses the importance of liking who you are in relation to your partner. This process is crucial in creating and maintaining a healthy intimacy. Rather than criticizing and name-calling, look inside yourself and identify what needs are not being adequately managed. We'll show you later in this chapter how you can actively identify, legitimatize, and represent your needs to your partner. When we do this, we are creating love for ourselves and our partners. We are learning how to self-generate love.

Before reading any further, take a moment and do a quick self-examination on your need management style. Does your partner provoke you to see things in yourself you'd rather not face? Do you blame your partner for not gratifying your needs? Has your passion diminished, or do you have a growing resentment of your partner? Do you have a chronic loss of affection for your partner, or have you fallen out of love? If you answered yes to any of these questions, then you need to study and apply the principles of this model.

Before we get to the nuts and bolts of the model, let's open the therapist's file cabinet and create a fictional case based upon a composite profile. This case will help preview several major points of the model.

## A Case Illustration

David would like to make love tonight, but his wife, Sharon, is still upset over their latest argument. David senses her coolness and attempts to sweet-talk her with gestures of kindness, which Sharon has come to detest. David's repair efforts include caressing and sexual come-ons that Sharon has grown to hate. Sharon thinks David's quick-fix methods ignore her deeper feelings and the need to talk things through.

David thinks sex is the best way to reduce tension and regain emotional closeness with Sharon. But Sharon does not enjoy making love to him when they are in the middle of an unresolved fight. Sharon enjoys sex, but only when she feels cared for and understood.

With this brief sketch in mind, let's bring David and Sharon onto the "therapeutic couch" and analyze their problem using the new model.

**David:** I'm angry with her because last night I wanted to get close to her and make love, but she was cold and distant.

**Sharon:** I'm sick and tired of him acting like a little baby when he doesn't get his way. He always tries to pretend like everything is okay when I am still upset.

**Therapist:** Sharon, it sounds like you were angry at David because he was coming on to you instead of talking things through. David, you seem hurt because Sharon rejected you when all you wanted to do was get close to her. Actually, I don't see anything wrong with what each of you wanted. David, do you see anything wrong with what Sharon needed?

**David:** No.

**Therapist:** Sharon, do you see anything wrong with David's desire to be close?

**Sharon:** No. I guess it was just his timing.

**David:** Well, when I stop and think about it, I guess I am sorry I blew up at her. I just wish I knew what to do when she upsets me like this.

**Therapist:** David, I like your honesty. Let's see if it would help to take the problem a step further. Have you thought of what your feelings might be telling you about yourself at the point when Sharon first said "No"?

**David:** I felt like I wasn't wanted. And when I get like that, I just want to strike back.

**Sharon:** I didn't realize he felt that way. He never shares his feelings.

**Therapist:** Sharon, it sounds like you'd like to know more about David's feelings. You've identified another important need. And David, when you feel like you are not wanted, what do you suppose this reveals about you?

**David:** I don't know. Maybe it's just that I get angry too easily. When I think Sharon is rejecting me, I mean.

**Sharon:** I feel closer to you now when you talk about what you really feel. I didn't know I made you feel unwanted. I just wanted to talk and resolve things first.

**Therapist:** David, what are you feeling right now?

**David:** When she talks that way, I feel like she wants to understand me.

**Therapist:** After listening to both of you, it seems you have identified some perfectly legitimate needs. David, what I suggest you consider next is how you might best represent your need to be close to Sharon. Sharon, the same thing applies to you. How could you effectively represent your need to be understood by David? Let's start with David, if that's okay with you, Sharon.

**Sharon:** Sure, that's fine.

**Therapist:** David, the first step in need representation involves balancing self and other respect. One of the ways you can do this is by asking Sharon for a moment of her time. Showing Sharon immediate respect credits you with the right to be understood. Next, you must express the need (to make love) and the deepest feelings associated with your need (closeness and love). This creates greater connection within yourself and with Sharon.

While this approach may increase the chances of need gratification, it should not be your highest priority. Instead, your efforts ought to be directed at the effective management of your need. This should be your biggest concern. In this way, you are self-generating love for you and your partner. And you are not dependent on Sharon's response in order to feel good about yourself and her.

## A Case Analysis

Let's stop the dialog now and explain some of the core features of the model. First, the therapist encourages David and Sharon to stop blaming each other. Blaming fans the fires of anger. More importantly, blaming prevents David and Sharon from effectively identifying, legitimatizing, and representing their needs.

Next, the therapist guides David and Sharon on how their intimate relationship reveals their individual needs. For example, the therapist shows how Sharon's rejection of David's efforts to repair their relationship hurt his feelings. Sharon's rejection reveals one of David's personality weaknesses ("I felt unloved"). Then the therapist suggests that David look inside himself and identify his need (physical intimacy).

In the process of guiding David and Sharon on how to identify their needs, the therapist also makes the point that their needs are legitimate. The therapist reinforces this point by prompting both David and Sharon to verbally acknowledge and validate each other's individual needs. David validates the legitimacy of Sharon's needs, and Sharon validates the legitimacy of David's needs. Instead of blaming, Sharon and David are now learning to respect themselves and each other.

Lastly, the therapist guides David on how he can effectively represent his need to make love with Sharon. He points out the steps of need representation. The therapist begins by stressing first the importance of balancing self and partner respect. The next step requires that David express his need and the deepest feelings associated with it. This deepens David's connection to himself and elevates the possibility of an intimate connection with Sharon.

The steps involved in effective need management show David and Sharon the priority of need management over immediate need gratification. They learn to make the quality of their relationship the highest priority.

Now let's go over all of the principles of the model.

# Principles of the Model

## Intimacy Reveals

Intimacy is the most powerful relationship. It opens us up like a surgeon's scalpel, revealing all of our flaws, foibles, and imperfections. For this reason, it should not be compared to any other type of relationship. It is in a league of its own.

The first principle of the model is that our intimate partners reveal who we are. They know us like no one else. Intimacy reveals us and makes us vulnerable and easily hurt. Intimacy delivers an unlimited number of close encounters in which the developed and not-so-developed parts of our personalities come under the spotlight. And there is no room to hide.

## What Gets Revealed?

So what do our intimate partners reveal about us? On the positive side, our partners bring out our emotional maturity: our strengths, compassion, virtues, and abilities. For example, a grieving husband who has lost a parent to cancer discovers the depth of his wife's compassion and support. When our positive qualities surface, we rarely experience conflict in our relationships.

However, our greatest challenges occur when our partners reveal what has yet to be developed in our own characters. None of us enters our intimate relationships fully mature. We all carry "emotional baggage" from our childhoods. Our partners do more than simply observe these defects. They often activate them. For example, one partner's tendency to control sets in motion the other partner's inclination to play a passive role.

Unfortunately, nothing brings out our emotional immaturity more starkly than conflict. Painfully for us, our weaknesses go under the spotlight. We are revealed for the developmental deficits of our childhoods. However, every time the argumentative heat is turned up, we have another chance to take a deeper and more comprehensive look at ourselves.

Consider what can happen when a husband reacts strongly to his wife's criticism that he is not helping enough with the children. Regrettably, she activates his defenses (he withdraws), his sensitivity to criticism (he gets hurt), and his deepest fears (he is inadequate and unlovable). The wife's criticism reveals her husband's developmental deficiencies. Under these circumstances, he readily feels hurt and unloved. At this point, the husband has an opportunity for self-examination of the kind that will ultimately enable him to identify and manage what his wife reveals about him.

Intimacy also reveals how effectively we manage the personal needs we bring to our partners. Unmet or mismanaged needs induce conflict and tension between partners. Conversely, well-managed needs enhance not only self-esteem, but also our partners' esteem for us. In the previous example, the criticized husband must identify and manage his needs for his wife's respect and encouragement when it comes to increasing his care of the children.

### Reactions

Once our partners have revealed something about us, how do we typically behave? If our partners' feedback is positive, there is no issue. We react favorably. However, when our partners provoke strong negative feelings, our reactions take one of three forms.

*First,* we may attempt to minimize or avoid the conflict. While this tactic produces an immediate relief of tension, it comes at the cost of leaving the problem unaddressed and likely to reoccur.

*Second,* if we feel too vulnerable or hurt, we may over-comply with our partners. We assume a passive role and under-represent our own needs. We try to please our partners at the expense of our own interests.

*Third,* if we don't like what our partners reveal about us, we may try to persuade our partners in order to get them to comply with us. If they agree, there is no conflict. If they disagree, there is tension, and we attempt to coerce them into taking our point of view.

What is your relationship revealing about you? How do you react? Do you run away? Do you give in? Do you try to change your partner? Do you blame your partner?

## Blaming: Inevitable and Destructive

When our partners disagree with us, frustrate us, or otherwise provoke us, it is natural to defend ourselves by blaming. Whether we avoid, fight back, give in, or attempt to persuade our partners, some form of blaming typically accompanies the conflict. It is the quickest and most immediate defense against the pain of being revealed. It takes the heat off ourselves and places it squarely on our partners. We view our partners as the cause of our negative feelings. They have failed to gratify our needs.

When we blame our partners, we are telling a *negative story* about them. Storytelling makes our partners responsible for failing to gratify our needs. It also relieves us of the difficult task of looking within ourselves and managing our own needs.

On the surface, blaming is always destructive. It ignites argumentative heat. Partners throw verbal darts at each other. In the moment, animosity prevails; we create an ambiance of hostility. We infuriate our partners and distance ourselves. We occupy an emotional cul-de-sac where little, if anything, gets resolved, and worse, everything potentially becomes inflamed. Our attention gets focused upon the details of what our partners are doing wrong. We are blind to our own feelings and needs and the most effective means of managing them. We become partner-directed. If our needs are frustrated or denied, it's their fault.

### Analyzing Our Stories

It is virtually impossible to stop blaming. The infinite demands, hurts, and frustrations of intimacy guarantee that all of us at some time or another will blame our partners. Further, our negative stories of our partners are often very accurate, or seem justifiable, which in turn reinforces our tendency to blame. However, we advocate an alternative.

We should take the time to analyze the stories we tell about our partners. What is this story really revealing about *me?* Be aware that we cannot tell a story about a partner without simultaneously telling a story about ourselves. For example, if I blame my partner for being "controlling," then what is this revealing about me? Exactly what am I doing, or more precisely, not doing, that makes it possible for me to be "controlled"? Am I under-representing my needs because I am afraid of an argument or a fight? Would I blame my partner if my own needs were being effectively managed? We don't think so. In short, by examining what our stories mean, we take the first step toward understanding our own mismanaged needs.

What negative stories do you tell about your partner? What do these stories reveal about you? What are your mismanaged or unmet needs?

## Need Management

Poor need management lays the groundwork for blame. Frustrated that our partners don't always gratify our needs, we attach labels to them like *selfish, uncaring,* and so on. We might even find ourselves creating elaborate stories that dig into our partners' backgrounds for explanations that fault them for their insensitivities. When they fail us, we feel justified in criticizing or even attacking them. In effect, what we have done is make our partners ultimately responsible for satisfying our needs.

Good need management requires that we look within ourselves and not to our partners. Just like ideal parents identify and manage their children's needs, we need to apply the same process to ourselves. We must become our own parents. This means we identify, legitimatize, and represent our own needs.

Consider how much easier it is to blame your partner than manage your own needs. How well do you manage your needs? Do you believe your partner is responsible for gratifying them? If so, what is the net result of thinking this way? If you've experienced disappointment, consider an alternate point of strategy—effective need management.

### Need Identification

The first step of effective need management is to identify our personal needs. This can be accomplished through direct and honest self-examination. For example, we can ask, what are my feelings? And what need(s) are activating these feelings? Intimate partners are continuously triggering each other's needs, often more than one at the same time. Very quickly things can get quite complex, requiring that we identify those needs we deem of highest importance.

We can also decipher our personal needs by analyzing the stories we tell about our partners. Embedded in every story are our own unmet or mismanaged needs. It is exactly these needs that ought to be identified and then actively managed.

For example, if I blame my partner for being a "controller," I am also telling a story about myself—as being "controlled." By analyzing my story, I will be able to dig out my own mismanaged or unmet needs.

The value of need identification is that it sharpens and defines who we are in relation to our partners. We have a clearer sense of our own identities, and with this comes an increase in our integrity and self-esteem.

When your partner provokes you, what feelings and needs are activated? In other words, what are your unmet or mismanaged needs?

### Need Legitimization

Need identification is a vital first step, but is not sufficient. We must also legitimatize our needs. This means we imbue our needs with positive self-talk that is supportive and accepting. Most, if not all, of our fundamental needs are perfectly legitimate, and we should view them in a positive light. They are neither right nor wrong. It is the poor management of our needs that creates tension and conflict in our relationships.

To illustrate the process of need legitimization, let's review the previous example and apply the principle. The sequence goes like this: The spouse stops blaming her partner for being controlling and instead looks inside herself and identifies her unmet needs. She identifies a perfectly legitimate need for calm, rational discussion with her husband. This positive reinterpretation of her experience deepens the legitimacy of her need and empowers her to effectively represent it

Even though our personal needs are basically legitimate and important, this does not entitle us to gratify them by any means at our disposal. Good need management never includes demands, manipulation, or attacking our partners.

Do you believe your needs are legitimate? Do you accept them? How well do you instill them with positive self-talk?

### Need Representation

Up to this point, need management is characterized by two mental processes. Specifically, need identification and need legitimization involve self-examination and the affirmation of our needs. Now, we involve our partners. Our goal is to effectively express our needs to our partners while showing respect for them at the same time.

We demonstrate respect for ourselves by identifying and legitimatizing our personal needs. Respect for our partners can be shown in a number of ways. When possible, we recommend asking our partners for a moment of their time, especially as a prelude to representing important needs. This clears the conversational ground and respects our partners' ongoing concerns or expectations in the moment. We can also convey respect for our partners by anticipating the effects that meeting our needs may have upon them. By showing our partners respect first, we pave the way for them to show respect for us.

Now that we have shown respect for our partners, we are ready to actively represent our personal needs. We do this by directly expressing our need(s) to our partners. We define, explain, or otherwise make plain just what our needs are and what it would mean to us if our partners were to gratify them.

This next point is equally important. Connected to every significant need are strong feelings. It is crucial that we speak from these deepest feelings. In effect, we are communicating two things:

the need itself, and the deepest feelings associated with the need. Can you begin to feel how difficult this could be?

Consider an example. A wife who is overworked at her company needs her husband's support with the care of their children. How she manages her need is critical. One option is that she might place an angry demand on her husband: "You've got to help more with the children. I'm doing all the work." This option is quick and easy, but it is poor need management. While her need is perfectly legitimate, she manages it by being defensive and demanding. She is not connecting with her deeper and more vulnerable feelings, nor is she showing respect for her husband.

A better option is for her to identify her need and the deepest feelings connected to it. This is more effective need management. She might say instead, "I'm a little afraid to ask you for your help. But I would feel cared for if you could help me more with the kids. I would feel like we were partners. In the past, when you've helped out, it's meant the world to me."

By making the much harder effort to explain to her husband what his support would mean, she makes a more complete and deeper connection with herself. Now her husband is in a better position to connect with her. He can understand his own contribution to the care of the children and its positive effect on his wife. This would not have been possible had the wife chosen a simpler approach.

When we express our personal needs and the deepest and most vulnerable feelings associated with them, we create a deep, meaningful connection within ourselves. This will elevate the possibility of a better connection with our partners. Don't expect this to be easy, because this part of the process involves the disclosure of our sensitive and vulnerable feelings. However, the rewards for doing so are enormous. Intimacy with ourselves makes possible a deeper intimacy with our partners.

Our efforts to effectively represent our personal needs must be evaluated by what we do, not by how our partners respond. It's natural to focus on our partners' reactions, hoping for a positive outcome (need gratification). But this very understandable tendency directs our attention onto our partners and off of ourselves. This means our self-management gears spin in neutral and we are left as passive agents. Remember, we do not have absolute control over our partners. Nor would we really want it. It is challenging enough to learn control over our own needs (need management).

This next point is also significant. The effective management of our personal needs must be a higher priority than whether or not we immediately gratify them. This may seem counter-productive, but as important as need gratification is, there is much more to be gained from effectively managing our needs. Again, for emphasis: *the benefits derived from effective need management far exceed the gains of immediate need gratification.*

So what do we gain? We gain self-respect and esteem for our partners. Think about it: identifying our personal needs defines who we are in relation to our partners. Making the effort to legitimatize our personal needs strengthens both our self-esteem and our resolve to represent them. Assertively expressing our needs and the deepest feelings connected to them while balancing respect for our partners not only deepens intimacy with ourselves, but also with our partners. Most importantly, the focus on how we manage our needs places the ongoing health of our relationship in a position of highest priority. It makes the immediate gratification of our personal needs secondary.

The result of effective need management is that we like who we are in relation to our partners. Consequently, we like our partners too. Remember, by prioritizing effective need management, we place self and partner respect and the health of the relationship above the immediate gratification of our personal needs. As you can see, the rewards of effective need management far outweigh the benefits of immediate need gratification.

Ironically, by focusing on how well we are managing our needs, we actually increase the possibility of gratifying them. Partners who respect each other are more likely to satisfy each other's needs. Good need management defines who we are in relation to one another and encourages self and partner respect, which in turn deepens mutual understanding. The resulting collaboration forces a shift in how we think about ourselves in relation to our partners: If I love who I am when I'm with you, then I love you too.

Effective need management generates love. Using our previous example, the passive partner might say, "I'd like a few moments of your time to talk about something very important to me that may have some effect on you. I don't often express my needs clearly, but I'd like to change that, and I think it will be better for both of us."

Notice that the passive partner is now effectively managing her needs. She focuses upon what she can control instead of worrying about whether her needs will be immediately gratified. This will reduce the anxiety associated with anticipating her partner's response, and managing her need will become easier.

Remember, effective need management always includes balancing respect for ourselves and for our partners. This means she should anticipate the effects of her actions on her spouse. She needs to take him into consideration.

Referring again to the example, the passive partner's success is gauged exclusively by reference to how she behaves. Through effective representation of her needs, this formerly passive partner respects herself more in relation to her partner. This increase in her self-respect allows her to experience greater love for her partner. And in turn, her partner's love for her will grow.

How well do you express your needs to your partner? Do you anticipate the impact your needs will have on your partner? When you represent your needs, do you also express the deepest feelings associated with them? Do you place the health of the relationship above the immediate gratification of your needs?

## Viewing Our Partners in a New Way

Effective need management creates a shift in our thinking about how we see ourselves in relation to our partners. This shift may require some adjustment in your thinking. Try to be flexible.

Let's suppose that you fall in love with your partner in large part because of his or her physical attributes (handsomeness or beauty). Now, what happens to your love when these qualities change? If your love is based primarily on your partner's traits, then you can expect your love to also change when these qualities inevitably shift. On the other hand, if your love is more deeply based on how you manage yourself in relation to your partner, then you will have greater control over how you create and maintain love.

Good need management means that we examine and manage how we think, feel, and behave toward our partners. When we manage ourselves well, we generate feelings of self-respect. Then we like who we are in relation to our partners. The end result is that we love our partners more. Let's explore an example of how good need management can work.

### A Case Example

Before becoming a psychologist, one of the authors worked as an administrator at a residential facility for developmentally disabled children. This is how he describes his experience:

"Part of my job duties involved transferring children who required more intensive care at other hospitals or facilities. What aroused my curiosity was the tearful reactions of some of the caregivers when the children were transferred. I was astonished that they could love children that seemingly had so little to give. Many of the children were so low functioning they could hardly control the drool at the corners of their mouths, and yet the caregivers loved these children! It seemed to me their love was not based on the qualities these children possessed; rather, it was based primarily on how they related to the children. Watching the caregivers interacting with the children was an inspiration to me."

Let's analyze the behavior of the caregivers. The manner in which the caregivers related to the children generated their positive feelings for them. For example, their initial impressions of the children might have ranged anywhere from compassion to indifference, or to repulsion and disgust. But these feelings were managed. For instance, the caregivers might have said, "These children need help, and we can help them."

Through their acting compassionately, three things occurred: first, the caregivers liked the kind of people they were when they were caring for the children. This increased their self-respect. Second, as caregivers they liked who they were when they were with the children; therefore, they liked the children. Third, any inherently likeable qualities in the children would have been amplified by the respectful care they were provided.

How might you have responded to these kids? How you think about others affects your feelings for them. How do you think about yourself in relation to your partner? How does this affect your feelings?

## Character-Based Love

This simple example points up the differences between *character-based love* and *self-generated love.* To review, character-based love means that we love others based on their traits or unique qualities. Self-generated love means that we love our partners based on what we are like when we are with them. Because these concepts are complex and central to the model, we are going to discuss them in greater detail in the next two sections.

Character-based love means that we love others for the traits in their characters. These qualities are viewed as the source of or explanation for our love. We literally mean, "I love her or him because she or he is 'kind,' 'confident,' witty,' 'fun,' 'sexy,' etc." This is the usual way we "fall in love" with each other. However, there is a major problem with it. Our love is dependent upon factors outside our personal control.

For example, let's refer to one type of male-female relationship. Suppose a woman loves a man primarily because of his income and the security this provides. This may be sufficient to maintain her affections until the man loses his job. Then what happens to her love? In this case, her love is based on qualities that are potentially changeable and outside her control. She cannot ensure his job security and therefore, her love for him.

In reality, most of us fall in love for a variety of reasons, some of which are more enduring than others. However, even the seemingly permanent qualities of character, such as intelligence or personality, are subject to change over the course of a lifetime. One obvious example is what happens to all of us as we get older. As we age, we change in a number of ways. There is a loss of energy, development of disease, and transformation of our values. Some of the changes we undergo radically alter our personalities. In the extreme, think about the changes that occur with diseases like cancer and Alzheimer's disease.

However, the changes we observe in ourselves and our loved ones don't always require dramatic events, the ravages of disease, or the transformations that occur over long periods of time. Consider a top executive who commands thousands of workers with his decision-making abilities, but at home he has trouble locating a pair of matching socks. Understandably, his wife is confused. She is attracted to his business intelligence but is put off by his lack of common sense. Character-based love is changeable, and the end result is a diminished capacity to genuinely love.

Ultimately, character-based love rests upon the shifting ground of our perceptions. Our love is based on how we view our partners' qualities. And as we have said, our view of our partners is subject to change.

Here's another common example: A love-struck young man describes his new girlfriend as "sexy and playful." After two years of marriage, however, he views these same qualities in an entirely new light. What he once perceived as sexy and playful is now seen as "irresponsible and immature." His love has changed because his perception of his wife's qualities has changed.

Unfortunately, character-based love is limiting and can even be destructive. One day we love our partners for their character traits; the next day we despise them for the very same traits. Character-based love is fickle. It changes with our perceptions and moods. It also varies as a consequence of how our partners manifest their traits.

As a graduate student, one of the authors told a friend that when he married it would be to an intelligent, educated woman— character-based love. He met and eventually married a fellow doctoral student. While her education and intelligence have contributed significantly to their relationship, they have also posed the greatest challenges. Sometimes these same traits are used in ways that outwit the author and undermine his arguments or weaken his logic (his problem).

What do you love about your partner? Is your love character-based? Has your view of your partner's qualities changed? If so, what has happened to your feelings about your partner? Is the love you feel now for your partner under your own control?

## Self-Generated Love

Self-generated love is robust and enduring. This is because it involves your internal source of control. It is self-generated rather than partner-generated. This is the reverse of the conventional thinking about love. Self-generated love means that we create and maintain our love for our partners by how we think, feel, and behave toward them. In this way, we are more in control of the love we feel for our partners. Our love is less dependent upon the qualities in their characters, and more dependent upon how *we* act toward our partners.

Self-generated love puts us in the driver's seat. Now, two very significant things happen: First, we generate love for our partner by how effectively we manage our needs. The result is we like ourselves more. This is one of the expected by-products of good need management. Second, because we like ourselves in relation to our partners, we feel better about them. We find our partners more enjoyable and fulfilling.

Even under very difficult circumstances, we can maintain our love for our partners by how well we manage our negative feelings. John Gottman, a preeminent researcher on marriage, has observed that couples who can manage negative emotions report greater satisfaction in their marriages. In fact, managing negative feelings allows us to like ourselves more. And when we like ourselves more, we are in a position to like our partners more too. Good need management is the key to self-generated love.

Let's go back to the caregiver example. Why were the caregivers able to love the children in spite of their disabilities? On the surface, it would not seem easy to love these children. They did not have the expected or normal personality characteristics. Nor were they capable of the normal give and take of relationships. Instead, it was how the caregivers saw themselves in relation to the children, and what they did for the children that would explain their love. In other words, they liked who they were in relation to the children. As a consequence, they loved and respected the children as well. Their love of the children was under the caregivers' control. It was self-generated.

## Application

Self-generated love is a difficult concept to understand. Let's look at it from a different angle. Imagine your spouse is very angry and is attacking you for something she or he thinks you've done wrong. Your need for self-respect has just been violated. Now, consider three possible responses: One, you protect yourself and counterattack with equal strength. Two, you withdraw and say nothing. Stop and analyze these first two responses. What do you feel? What is gained? What is lost? What happens to your self-esteem? As you may have guessed, these are examples of poor need management. The result of these types of need management is predictable: you feel worse about yourself and your partner.

This leaves us with the third response. Consider trying something more difficult, or even completely unnatural. Focus on your own reactions (hurt, anger) and manage them in a way that leaves you feeling greater self-respect. This includes evaluating your efforts by what you do, not by how your partner responds. By doing this, you can be successful regardless of how your partner reacts to you.

For example, you might say, "When my feelings build up, I don't always resolve things the way I'd like to. I need to calm down and then deal with this problem later." Note that there's no blaming, counterattacking, or avoiding the problem. Instead, there's a thoughtful and deliberate attempt to manage needs and feelings in the most effective and respectful way possible.

The point is this: as we manage ourselves in a respectful way, we view ourselves and our partners more positively. Further, we no longer have to feel like a victim of our partners' lack of affection, inconsideration, or worse, their cruelty. We are therefore able to nurture and preserve the love we have for our partners by managing what we have most control over—ourselves.

Consider how you might self-generate love in your own life. One of the authors challenges himself in the following way:

"When I come home to my wife, my feelings for her ought to be self-generated and under my control, rather than character-based over which I have no control. My hope is for a kind, warm greeting. While such a greeting would be nice, it may not always be realistic. When I am aware of how I am feeling and manage these feelings, then I can be more in control of how I experience my love for her at that moment. If she's tired or distant, would I really want her mood to negatively affect me? By contrast, when I manage myself, I safeguard my feelings and as a result, I am better able to create feelings of love for her. In short, when I respect what I am when I am around her, I love her."

In the last section, we asked you what type of love you have for your partner. Now, consider if it is primarily character-based or self-generated. If it is character-based (remember, character-based love is based upon your partner's personality traits), has your love changed? Do you see your partner's traits the same way today as you did when you first met? Can you recall times when your love was self-generated? If so, how did you feel? Did you feel better about yourself? Did you feel better about your partner? Did your partner feel better about you?

## Change Ourselves and Change Our Relationships

Learning how to be effective need managers does more than increase the respect we have for ourselves and our partners. It improves our relationships. Effective need managers bring out the best in their partners. Our partners act less defensively, show greater caring and support, and respond to us more respectfully. Our partners now become powerful sources of feedback that positively impacts the way we feel about ourselves. As you can see, effective need management brings out the best in ourselves and our partners. The bottom line is that our partners' positive regard for us enhances our own self-respect.

Let's clarify these complex ideas with an example. One of the authors describes a family conflict between himself, his wife, and his recently married daughter. In his words:

"I guess I felt a little jealous and maybe even competitive with my daughter because of all the time she demanded of my wife. I felt like I was being pushed aside. I was angry with my wife for giving in to my daughter's demands, and I resented my daughter for intruding on our privacy.

"What I discovered was that having been adopted as a young child left me with a hollow feeling about belonging. It made it difficult to experience typical family bonding...like there was a missing piece. My motivation to be close to each of them forced me to reconsider the way I saw their relationship. Some careful reflection helped me to see that my wife was simply trying to be the best mother she could be, and my daughter was frightened of letting go of our family. With this altered perception, I began to enjoy them together. And because of my new feelings, they saw me as more lovable. They acted more positively about me, and as a result I felt better about myself."

Again, when you manage yourself well, how do you feel? Do you feel more self-respect? How do you feel about your partner? How does your partner feel about you?

## Intimacy Is the Best Vehicle for Change and Growth

The intimate relationship is incomparable. It reveals us like no other relationship. Our partners come to know us thoroughly and are in a position to provoke intense feelings of conflict, frustration, and hurt. Of course, we also experience positive feelings too, but these don't require the same type of need management.

Intense negative feelings are like windows into the deficiencies of our development. For example, a wife who as a child witnessed her parents' violent fighting cannot tolerate even the prospect of disagreement with her husband. Consequently, she finds it difficult to assert her needs out of fear that she'll provoke an argument.

Intimacy reveals the deficiencies of our development. It provides a special context in which the underdeveloped parts of ourselves get drawn into the open. The good news is that once these parts of ourselves are revealed, we can understand and manage them. We can further our growth and development and enhance our intimate relationships. However, if we ignore these revealed underdeveloped parts, then our weaknesses interfere with the quality of our relationships. Worse, they can even destroy the relationships.

By effectively managing what our intimate partners reveal about us, we build self-esteem. For every effort at improved need management, there is a corresponding increase in the respect we feel for ourselves and the respect our partners have for us. The love we receive from our partners is equal to the quality of our need management. That is, we can directly influence the love our partners have for us by how well we manage the personal needs we bring to our partners.

Remember, too, we can be no more intimate with our partners than we are intimate with ourselves. No other type of relationship offers us these opportunities for growth as profoundly and consistently. What does your spouse teach you about yourself? How have you grown as a result of this feedback? If you have grown, how has this affected your relationship?

## The Long and Short of Need Management

The model we've just covered represents the longhand version of effective need management. And you've probably noticed, it may seem tedious, difficult, or overly formal. "Oh, honey, do you have a moment so that we can talk? I have an important need to manage." Who speaks this way?

It's true that applying all of the steps of need management requires that we invest time and energy in our relationships. However, life can get urgent and rushed, leaving us little or no time to apply all the steps of effective need management. Fortunately, many of the steps of the model can be modified so that shorthand versions of need management can be used in a pinch when time is at a premium.

For example, imagine that you and your partner are racing out the door to get to a party. You are aware of your partner's excitement and that your partner wants to stay at the party longer than you do. Now, picture yourself making a quick bid for compromise by saying, "Since you enjoy spending more time at these activities than I normally do, what if we were to spend tomorrow night at the movies, and I'll stay with you as long as you'd like at tonight's party?" This very recognizable effort at compromise is simple, to the point, and yet still contains some of the basics of good need management.

Compromise implies we have identified our needs and legitimatized them, and that we show respect for ourselves and our partners. These steps are quick and efficient. Further, they can open the door to more complete need management and the full array of its benefits.

Even everyday considerations like "Please" and "Thank you" represent some of the simplest forms of effective need management. As short as they are, these common courtesies contain a healthy dose of self and other respect, need identification, and need representation. For example, when one partner thanks another for an act of kindness, both are being respected. And in a very short form, needs and feelings are being identified and represented.

There are obvious advantages to shorthand versions of need management. During times of urgency, they are quick and to the point. The disadvantage is that all of the benefits that come with complete need management cannot be realized. To obtain the full array of benefits, time and energy must be invested in each of the steps of the model.

## Summary of the Model

Congratulations! You have just survived some very complex ideas. Let's break these concepts down into a few easy to remember steps.

## Intimacy Reveals Us

Intimacy opens us up. It exposes all of our strengths and weaknesses. If we choose to be intimate, these revelations are unavoidable. Without doubt, the most difficult revelations involve the underdeveloped parts of our characters. When these deficiencies of our characters come glaringly to light, they must be managed.

## Managing What Is Revealed

We must learn to manage what our partners reveal about us. Our partners ultimately see our deficiencies in some form or another. If we defensively hide or ignore our weak spots, intimacy suffers. Ideally, our partners shouldn't be the victims of those parts of us that are not fully developed. Nor should they be held responsible for them. We have the responsibility to know and then correct our own weaknesses.

## Managing Our Needs

Intimacy requires that we effectively manage the needs we bring to our relationships. Of course, this means that we identify, legitimatize, and represent our needs. These processes are central to self-generated love.

Need identification defines who we are in relation to our partners. It helps build self-esteem. Need legitimization imbues the need with acceptance and the impetus for actively representing it. Need representation expresses the identified need. It reveals the feelings associated with it. At the same time, it creates a balancing of self and partner respect. The effective management of our needs means that we are generating love for ourselves and our partners. *We are literally making love.*

Self-generated love permeates the entire relationship. It places the health of the relationship above the immediate gratification of personal needs.

## Application of the Model

This model has a broad application. It extends beyond its use in psychotherapy. It addresses everyday needs and issues to be found in all couple relationships. Consider the following possibilities:

- **Diminished passion for one's partner** It is common knowledge that partners meet, fall deeply and passionately in love, and then gradually lose their passion for each other as the relationship develops and changes over time. Our model explains not only why this happens, but what can be done to prevent and/or correct it (see Chapter Three).

- **Conflicts and arguments over various life issues** Conflicting individual needs over money, sex, child-rearing, etc., commonly plague the intimate relationship. Our model prescribes exactly what conflicting partners can do to deepen mutual respect and understanding. The model shows how to manage differing needs and grow self and partner esteem (see Chapters Four, Five, and Six).

- **The problem of extramarital affairs** If you are considering, or have already engaged in, an affair, we prescribe that you stop and examine yourself in terms of our model. What needs are not being effectively managed within your current relationship? The model teaches that affairs actually represent an escape from the self. Further, the model shows how our needs can be effectively managed. This can be done within the couple's intimate relationship, and so reduce the likelihood of an extramarital affair (see Chapter Seven).

- **The Problem of Divorce** If you are contemplating a divorce, we recommend that you reconsider your decision and apply the principles of the model. Frankly, some relationships should be terminated. But these are relatively few. Most troubled relationships can be repaired through the intervention and application of our model (see Chapter Eight).

# Personal Exercise

Let's personalize these ideas with an exercise you can try with your partner. Start by identifying a typical conflict. Once you've *found* a problem, go through the steps below. As you follow the steps, see if you can spot the differences between how you've handled this problem before and what happens now, when you apply the principles of good need management.

First, what does the identified conflict reveal about you? Second, look deep inside yourself and identify a need(s) that is being frustrated. How have you attempted to manage this need? Have you blamed your partner? Have you withdrawn from your partner? Of course, these are examples of poor need management.

Third, think of how you might manage the same need in a way that will build your self-respect. For example, suppose you want to be more emotionally intimate with your partner. However, you find your partner is non-responsive. What should you do? Start by defining what you need and expressing it to your partner. Do it in a way that leaves your partner with a non-pressured yes or no option. In other words, make a request, not a demand. Your efforts should involve balancing respect for yourself and your partner.

Fourth, measure your success by what you have tried to do, rather than whether your partner has gratified your need. Keep in mind there are many ways in which your need can be satisfied, but your highest priority is effective need management. How will you know if you are doing a good job? The best clue to your success will be feelings of greater self-respect. You will also feel more respect for your partner. In turn, your partner will feel more respect for you.

# Part II
# Building Lasting Relationships

# Chapter Three
# Love Under the Microscope

One of the authors, Robert Johansen, relates that at fifteen, passion hit him like a bolt of lightning. "Thoughts of my new girlfriend enveloped me. I couldn't get her out of my mind, nor did I want to. I remember exactly where I was and what I was doing when this wave of feeling swept over me. It was late afternoon, and as I walked around the corner on the street where I lived, I felt charged with energy and excitement. My senses were heightened. The sky was bluer, the sunlight slanting through the air was majestic. Everything around me appeared more vivid, alive, and meaningful. For a brief, glorious moment, nothing was wrong or could go wrong. The worth of my existence had been confirmed. Everything was perfect. I was in love."

## Romance vs. Marriage

We all know the feelings of romantic love are captivating, passionate, and exciting. But contrast these feelings with those associated with marriage. What do you discover?

In our intimacy workshops, we try to deepen an understanding of romantic love versus marriage by asking our audiences to free associate to the words "romance" and "marriage." To do this, we ask members of the audience to shout out the first thing that comes to mind when they think of these words. Before you look at how our audiences respond, give some thought to your own reactions to these words.

| Romance | Marriage |
|---|---|
| 1. Falling in Love | 1. Mature Love |
| 2. Sexy | 2. Duty |
| 3. Exciting | 3. Obligations |
| 4. Passionate | 4. Responsibilities |
| 5. Perfect | 5. Children |

| | |
|---|---|
| 6.  Flirtation | 6.  Family |
| 7.  Fantasy | 7.  In-Laws |
| 8.  Seductive | 8.  Commitment |
| 9.  Kissing | 9.  Security |
| 10. Dating | 10. Loss of Freedom |

Did you come up with any of these words? It's very likely your reactions were similar. Now, examine each list carefully and note the differences. As you can see, romance evokes thoughts of passion, excitement, and playfulness, whereas marriage makes us think of responsibilities and commitments. Clearly, marriage is a more complicated and difficult relationship.

Marriage is the most challenging relationship. However, it begins with little or no training, sometimes with just a quick burst of passion and excitement. At worst, the transition from the romantic phase to the complexities of marriage is left to sheer chance. At best, we are left with whatever example our parents provided. Because of this, many couples cannot make the difficult shift from romantic love to mature love.

First, let's study the highs and lows of romantic love so that we can better understand what we are up against. We'll see how romantic love both entices and betrays us.

## The Highs and Lows of Romantic Love

Reflect for a moment on your first romantic experience. Were you filled with passion? Did you feel more alive? Did you think your love was perfect? If you answered "yes" to any of these questions, you were probably experiencing romantic love.

Romantic love is an intoxicating high. It affirms our worth and builds our confidence. It fills our emptiness. We feel more alive. Passion pervades us. Suddenly, there is new meaning, purpose, and direction to our lives. The magic of romance sweeps us off our feet. Now, let's take a closer look at how we are seduced by the highs of romantic love.

**Romantic love is one of the most powerful forms of human connection.** It's more than simple attraction and sexual desire. According to Robert Sternberg, an expert on the psychology of love, romantic love is a combination of passion and intimacy. Passion is sexual desire and an intense longing for our partners. Intimacy is a deep, caring friendship. It involves a concern for our partners' well-being and a need to share experiences.

These intense emotions create a sense of unity. The heat of romance is like a welder's torch; it fuses us together. We are connected, and the experience is deep, complete, and extremely gratifying.

Do you recall feeling intense passion for your partner? Do you remember longing to be together? Do you recall the possessiveness and concern that go with being immersed in romantic love? Did you feel at one with your partner?

**Romantic love affirms us.** We search out all that we have in common and celebrate our sameness. Our partners confirm what we value; they share our ideals. What's important and meaningful to one partner is enthusiastically endorsed by the other. We want and aspire to the same things. Even our dreams of the future seem to co-mingle. Compatibility abounds. By virtue of these compatibilities, true romance affirms our worth and strengthens our self-esteem.

Do you recall how your romantic partner supported you? Did she or he see the world in the same or similar ways? Do you remember feeling like you and your partner were perfectly compatible?

**Romantic love provides a powerful incentive to strengthen our promises to each other.** Instead of being deterred by the fears of deeper commitment, romance persuades us to take on these responsibilities in spite of their burdens. We are moved to deepen our devotion through pledges, promises, engagement, and eventually marriage.

Do you remember being so much in love that you never wanted your passion to end? Did you try to preserve your excitement and passion by making a commitment to your partner?

**Romantic love is like a shot in the arm.** It boosts our self-esteem. We trust more, open up, and share our feelings. Romantic love makes us more confident in ourselves and our abilities. We raise the ceiling on our ambitions, goals, and sexual prowess. We go without food and sleep. In the throes of romance, we think we are capable of anything.

Do you remember feeling the jolt of romance? Do you remember the burst of confidence and energy? Do you recall feeling like you and your romantic partner could do anything together?

**Romantic love is inspiring.** Our culture is sizzling with the exciting music, cinema, and literature of romance. Romance breathes an invigorating dimension of warmth and meaning into our lives. We are enriched and made happy by it. We smile at the sight of a loving couple, or when we get the wedding announcement of a family member or friend. Romance enlivens and enhances us. It imparts new purpose to our lives. Without romance, life is less passionate and exciting.

Are you inspired by our culture's love affair with romance? Is romance a regular part of your life?

## The Lows

Have you ever been dumped? How did you feel? Do you remember saying to yourself, "I'll never fall in love again," but eventually you went ahead and did it anyway? What is so seductive about romantic love? Why do we put our hearts at risk? Why do we spend so much time, energy, and money pursuing it?

The answers to these questions are found in some of the compelling, but negative aspects of romantic love.

**Romantic love is short-lived.** Most of us know the splendors of a hot romance are hard to sustain. In fact, some experts think that frequent and prolonged separation is the only way to maintain romance. It is easier to keep a positive picture of someone if he or she is not around a lot. Romance cries out for togetherness, but unfortunately, continued closeness snuffs out romantic feelings. Romance is its own worst enemy.

Have you lost your romantic feelings for your partner? If so, how long did your feelings last? What became of them? Are they dead forever?

**Romantic love is an illusion.** It is a form of love that is based more on fantasy than reality. The fantasy comes from the fact that we don't thoroughly know our romantic partners. In the absence of knowing our partners, we make them into anything we need them to be. For a brief period of time, we bask in an illusion of compatibility. As a teenager, one of the authors felt his first love interest possessed all the qualities that would make him happy forever. Sadly, he did not know his girlfriend or himself that well. The relationship lasted five weeks. He confused fantasy with reality.

When you were in love, did you confuse fantasy with reality? Did you imagine your partner to be someone that he or she was not? After you really got to know your partner, did your illusions slowly disintegrate or shatter?

**Romantic love is child-like.** Romantic love promotes childlike tendencies. Have you ever whispered sweet nothings in your lover's ear? Or have you used pet names or baby talk to convey your feelings to your partner? Have you felt your I.Q. drop several points because love prompted you to say or do something stupid?

Even worse, we expect our partners to read our minds. They should know what we want and when we want it. After all, they love us, don't they? Similarly, our personal space and boundaries become blurred. If I like it, so must you. If I see it this way, you must see it this way too. There is no accommodating of personal differences. This stands at odds with mature love, in which individual differences are acknowledged and respected.

Have you ever felt childish in your relationship? Do you expect your partner to read your mind? Do you sometimes expect that just because you like something, your partner must like it too?

**Romantic love is like an illegal drug.** It hooks us quickly and deeply with feelings of euphoria. It is easy to become dependent on something or someone outside of ourselves. We become intoxicated, then addicted. We get fooled into thinking that our romantic partner is the source of our happiness.

Just as drugs seem to help us deal with our problems and fill the emptiness inside us, so does romantic love. However, both delude us. Each offers nothing more than a temporary fix for our problems. The quick highs give way to troublesome lows.

Have you ever felt addicted to someone? Did you feel attracted to this person, but at the same time knew he or she was not good for you? Even your friends thought you were an idiot. *But you* knew you were in love.

**Romantic love is inescapable.** Romantic love is woven deeply into our culture. Everywhere we look, romance is being pushed, promoted, or packaged in some form or another. We are bombarded with images of passionate love promising ecstasy and fulfillment. It is impossible to escape them. They are part of almost everything we read, see on television, and watch at the movies. In fact, romance is so much a part of our everyday lives that the only acceptable reasons for not pursuing it are disease and old age.

We live in a love culture, victimized by the false promises of romantic love. All we have to do is believe in the magic of love. This may sound silly, but think how easy it is for us to be seduced.

Do you feel bombarded with images of love? Have you ever felt something was missing in your life because you were not head-over-heels in love?

**Romantic love is heartbreaking.** Romance always courts the prospect of loss through competition with rivals, or the possibility that our partners may lose interest in us. To love is to risk heartache and pain. In fact, all relationships end. You break up, your partner dies, or you die. There are no other exceptions.

Sadly for some, romance is a deadly dance. There are too many tragic stories of jilted lovers who commit unspeakable crimes in the name of "love." For these perpetrators, the threat of or actual loss of a lover is intolerable. Unable to grieve their loss, they resort to harassment, stalking, or other criminal behavior, including murder and suicide.

How many times has your heart been broken? How far would you go in the name of love? Would you give up your job and move across the country to be with your lover? Would you become a stalker? Would you commit murder?

**Romantic love is character-based.** That is, we find qualities we like in our romantic partners and then fall in love. This is the usual way we begin a romantic relationship. But this can be devastating. For example, a woman falls madly in love with a handsome and charming man. She is intoxicated by his good looks and charisma. If these qualities are the main focus of her love, what might happen? Think about it. The qualities that fueled her initial attraction soon turn into a threat. She hates the fact that other women find him attractive too. She becomes insecure and is afraid of losing him. Her romantic love turns to jealousy. Is a breakup imminent?

Ironically, it is often the very same character traits we fall in love with that cause us to break up. A partner's good looks become a threat. A partner's confidence turns into dominance and control. A partner's keen intellect comes to be seen as a tool for deception and manipulation. Initial compatibilities convert to irreconcilable differences.

Equally ironic, we explain or justify our breakups by referring to character traits in our partners. We've all heard divorcing spouses say things like, "I never realized how selfish he could be," or "She was such a negative person, always angry about something." We tend to fall in and out of love on the basis of our partners' traits— often the very same traits!

There's another character-based twist to romantic love. We tend to be attracted to qualities in our romantic partners that were missing in our childhood. This includes things we wanted but never got. For instance, a young man is very attracted to his wealthy older girlfriend who seems to have it all. She drives a new model car, has elegant clothes, and always seems to have extra money to spend. Her wealth stands in contrast to his humble childhood, where every penny had to be stretched to make ends meet. He finds in her what is missing in himself.

What attracted you to your partner? Did you fall in love with him or her because of his or her qualities? Did these qualities change over time? Do you now find yourself hurt or frustrated by the same traits in your partner that you were once attracted to? Do the qualities you find attractive in a mate make up for something missing in your past?

## The Worst Low

The worst of the romantic lows is character-based love. This is why. If you look carefully, you can see the threads of character-based love running through each of the other lows. Embedded in every one is the notion that forces outside of ourselves create romantic love. For instance, romance takes on its addictive properties because of the belief that our partners are the ultimate source of our happiness. According to this way of thinking, it is our partners who fill our emptiness, solve our problems, and otherwise make us happy. This misconception, like the other deceptions of romantic love, eventually gets crushed.

At this point, let's tackle the origins of romantic love. We'll see how romantic love is character-based and flawed. We'll also examine the similarities between three types of love: *romantic, infantile,* and *character-based love.* Then in the closing section, we will cover how we can overcome the limitations of character-based love.

# The Origins of Romantic Love

Romantic love is extremely forceful in our lives. It affects us in many ways, both good and bad. Romance compels us to do things that are completely out of character, extreme things we wouldn't ordinarily do. We give up what's important to us, move away from parents, family, and friends. We sacrifice our independence and identity to be joined in romantic love. We might even step in front of a bullet to protect our romantic partners.

Few things exceed the force of romantic love. Where does this force come from?

## The Biology of Romantic Love

How would you like an example of high octane, in-your-face, revved-up sexuality and passion? Well, it's right under our noses. Look at the romantic behavior of a teenager. He or she is impulsive, wanton, immediate, and sometimes reckless. In the extreme, teen love leaves a wake of heartbreak, crushed confidence, and unwanted pregnancy. All of this unchecked sexual energy has its origins right at the very center of our brains.

An area called the limbic system regulates the basic emotions and hormones associated with sex and love. In other words, our brains are hard-wired for romantic love. Under the direction of the limbic system, the typical adolescent undergoes a surge of hormones that ready his or her body for sexual stimulation. At this stage of development, sexual responses are raw, disorganized, and under-regulated. Sex and love are hormone-charged. With the slightest stimulation, romantic love bursts onto the scene. The mere glimpse of a shapely leg, a confident smile, or baby-blue eyes is all it takes to launch our desires.

Fortunately, as the adolescent continues to develop, social and psychological pressures impose restraints on his or her raging hormones. Biology bends to social and psychological demands. Mature love finds a foothold as a shift occurs from hormone-based romance to the possibility for real intimacy.

## Infant Love

Actually, the origins of romantic love existed long before the rush of adolescent hormones. Its roots can be found in our earliest experiences, when we floated in the warm paradise of our mother's womb. Here, every creature comfort was indulged without asking, bargaining, or compromise. And, for a short time after our birth, life wasn't much different. We did nothing, and for the most part, our needs were met.

We stayed in a tight orbit around our mothers, where it was safest and most gratifying. There was something about her presence that made us come more alive, and something about her absence that made us anxious. As long as she remained within range, we felt a strength and security only she could provide. We acted with a natural spontaneity, expanding our range of play and our contact with the world. Knowing we could return to her for support, we ventured further into the enriching experiences awaiting us. This parent-child connection helped develop who we are.

This is infant love. It is our first relationship. Moreover, our earliest relationships are crucial because we want to repeat what was good about them and avoid what was bad. When things went as they should, we felt secure, safe, loved, and more alive. Without always being aware of it, we strive to repeat this critical early experience in our intimate relationships.

We've just described our first intimate relationship. In a nutshell, this is what it was like: We were dependent. We gave nothing and only received. There were no clear boundaries between ourselves and our mothers; we were enmeshed. Our parents were physically larger, more powerful, and dispensed vital supplies. We idealized them. We saw them as perfect. In their presence, we felt safer, confident, animated, and whole. Be sure and keep these points in mind, because they are also part of the feelings we have when we fall in love.

## Infant and Romantic Love

As strange as it may seem, infant love is strikingly similar to adult romantic love. These surprising resemblances are important to understand, because our earliest experiences of love influence how we expect to be loved as adults. With this in mind, take a closer look at the similarities between these two important forms of love.

**First, both relationships are dependent forms of loving.** They rely on external sources (other people) for feelings of well-being. The physical and emotional welfare of a baby hinges upon the care of its mother. A lover also looks to his or her partner as a primary source of emotional and physical nurturing. In both cases, the power to gratify is invested in other people.

**Second, both relationships are enmeshed.** There are no clear personal boundaries. An infant has no sense of individual identity apart from his or her mother. Both selves overlap. Later in childhood, their emotional merger can still be seen: If my mother is happy, so am I. Likewise, if my mother is happy with me, I am happy with myself. The emotional borders between lovers are equally blurry. We don't know where our partners begin and where we end. If my lover is happy, so am I. If my lover is pleased with me, I am pleased with myself. Again, the relationship is symbiotic.

**Third, both relationships are idealized.** In the infant's case, the mother is seen as perfect. Her position of total power makes her appear flawless. Her influence is absolute; she doles out rewards and punishments. She can do no wrong. Similarly, lovers put each other on a pedestal. They inflate their mate's positive traits while keeping a blind eye to their negative ones. The idealized partner assumes a position of power to reward or punish. Our romantic partners seem perfect.

**Fourth, both relationships enliven us.** In every sense, the mother brings life to her infant. The infant thrives under the quality of her care. The mother's touch, look, and softness breathe life, purpose, and meaning into the child's existence. Now, think of a couple smitten with romantic love. They are bubbly with joy. They are vivacious. Their lives suddenly swell with new meaning. Energy and optimism seem boundless. Romance brings us to life.

We've seen how romance is a throwback to our first experience of love. Maybe you can find these similarities in your own life. All of us know how an infant depends on his or her parents. Doesn't this also apply to lovers? They depend upon each other for emotional sustenance. Is this true for you?

## Romantic and Character-Based Love

In romance, we view the traits in our partners as the source of our love, the hallmark of character-based love. We romantically love our partners for whom we perceive them to be. We fall in love with them because of their "wonderful attributes." For example, "I love you because you possess a good sense of humor." Romantic love is character-based to the extent that we fall in love with the total package. We hope the package never changes.

### Character-Based Love

Refresh your memory for a moment while we review the basics of character-based love. This type of love derives from the qualities or characteristics found in our partners' personalities. Unfortunately, these qualities are likely to change or be seen differently at a later point in time. At best, it is a starting point for mature love. But it cannot be counted on to sustain long-term, intimate relationships. At worst, it breeds disillusionment, resentment, and contempt, the same feelings that accompany the demise of a relationship.

There are two types of character-based love. The first is infant love. The second is romantic love. Infant and romantic love are similar in the sense that each relies upon other people. With infant love, it is the parents who provide the nurturing. In the case of romantic love, it is our attraction to the personality traits in our partners that explains our feelings of love. In this sense, then, romantic love and infant love are character-based.

## Origins

Where does character-based love come from? We first recognize it in infancy. It is the first bond of love. Character-based love epitomizes the attachment between the infant and the mother. The infant is dependent upon the maternal capabilities of its mother.

The mother's resources are made available to the child, and development unfolds. If the mother fails to meet the infant's emotional needs, development is blocked. *The child's unmet needs are eventually carried forward into all other adult intimate relationships.* The child grows into an adult who becomes too dependent on his or her partner for emotional nourishment.

Here is a common example. Consider the case of a father who failed to provide adequate love to his daughter. As a teenager, the daughter finds herself drawn to her adolescent male friends. She is especially enticed by their flirtations and affections. Her infatuations are character-based. They are intended to make up for her father's lack of attention.

Here's a mental exercise that can help you bring personal meaning to this last point. Ask yourself what attracted you to your partner. Why were you attracted to these specific qualities? Your answers may give you valuable information about what was missing in your early relationships. Put simply, what we didn't get from our parents we often try to get from the next intimate relationship.

# The Language of Self-Generated Love

Let's review and deepen our knowledge of self-generated love. To start, here's a quick and easy definition: *If I like who I am when I am with you, then I like you too.* Our feelings hinge on what we do, not on what we expect or hope our partners will do. We learn to self-generate love. We put ourselves in control of what we feel for our partners.

Even under difficult circumstances, when our partners are doing things we don't like, we can still maintain our love for them through effective self-management. The essential question is: Do I respect who I am when I am with you? When the answer is yes, then we are in a better position to create and maintain love for our partners. When we like the kind of person we are when we are with our partners, then we grow our love for ourselves and our partners as well.

Conversely, when we don't like the kind of person we are when we are with our partners, then it will be very difficult to like our partners, especially over the long term. Remember, self-generated love is not dependent on the qualities in our partners. It is under our control; we create it. The beauty of this is, when we like ourselves in relation to our partners, we also like our partners.

While self-generated love can be practiced in any relationship, it has its hardest application in an intimate relationship. Think about why this is the case. Plainly, intimacy is the most difficult and complicated relationship. It reveals us. It activates our needs and wants. What do we do with what becomes revealed?

First, we make the decision to like the person we are in relation to our partner. This is a choice. It is under our control. Second, we identify, legitimatize, and effectively represent the needs we bring to our partners. Knowing what we need and managing it well creates self-respect and respect for our partners.

## Shifting Our Thinking

How do we advance from character-based love, which is trait dependent, to self-generated love, which is the product of our own effort? As we've shown, knowing what was missing in the first intimacy with our parents can be a big help. We must also learn the difficult lessons and limitations of character-based love. In short, our romantic partners aren't always what we'd like or need them to be. To make love more enduring, and to bring it under greater personal control, we must shift our thinking in some very important ways.

First, we must think of love as being our own creation instead of something we fall into or something that happens to us. Ordinarily, we assume that what we feel for our partners is directly related to their traits or behaviors. When our partners treat us well, we feel good. When they hurt us, we feel bad. We therefore make the very understandable but questionable assumption that our partners cause our feelings.

Now, try this little mental exercise on for size. The same behavior in our partner may bring different reactions at different times. For example, on one occasion your spouse's criticism is felt deeply and painfully. Yet on another occasion the very same criticism runs right off your back. Why such a dramatic difference? When the criticism runs off your back, you're effectively managing your needs (even though you may not be aware of it. You therefore feel better about yourself and your partner. Because you were feeling better about yourself, you were more immune to your spouse's criticism. What this example points out is that in the final analysis, *we create what we feel.*

This is a complex point, but it is important to understand its ramifications. By putting ourselves behind the helm of what we feel, we take greater control of our needs and the quality of our relationships. By the way, this is also consistent with the principles of good mental health.

## Benefits of Self-Generated Love

Self-generated love promotes the health of our relationships. It puts us in command of the love we feel for our partners. And the benefits are far-reaching.

First, we grow esteem for ourselves and our partners. Need identification, legitimization, and representation are the steps by which we construct ourselves. This process is similar to a muscle that's being defined and toned through regular physical exercise. And this is exactly what good parents do to build healthy self-esteem in their children. They identify, legitimatize, and help their children manage their needs.

Second, increased self-esteem boosts our passion for our partners. Typically, passion dies and romance fades. What has happened to your passion? Has it cooled? If it has, think about why. In the beginning of our relationships, passion springs from romance. Remember, romance is character-based. Romance is based on the perceived qualities in our partners' personalities. When these qualities change, romance and passion fade. There is little left to hold romance and passion in place.

But when we are more respecting of ourselves and our partners, we generate greater passion. A transition is made. Our desire is now under *our* control. Can you imagine having sustained, passionate sex with someone you do not respect?

Many factors, both physical and psychological, play into our sexual attraction for one another. The way our partners look and feel, what they say and do, what they accomplish, and the extent to which we feel emotionally connected to them are all part of what stimulates our sexual interest. However, the most stable sexual attraction is our own and our partners' self-esteem. It's the most powerful and lasting aphrodisiac!

Self-generated love improves the quality of our relationships. There are many ways we might evaluate the quality of an intimate relationship, but to our way of thinking, one of the best ways is to assess the individual maturity of each partner. The overall quality of intimacy can be no better than the level of maturity each partner brings to the relationship. Practicing the skills of self-generated love is an excellent way to strengthen maturity and build respect for ourselves and our partners.

## A Case Example

Jason's love for Jennifer is character-based. He fell in love with Jennifer's outgoing personality. She makes him feel more alive. Jennifer is a social butterfly. She's Jason's link to the outside world. What is character-based about Jason's love? It's the fact that Jason is dependent upon Jennifer's social skills.

Over the course of their relationship, Jason's dependency becomes a source of tension between the two of them. Every time he relies upon Jennifer to call friends, make plans, and in short, bail him out socially, Jason loses a little more self-esteem. In other words, he respects himself less, and this impacts his relationship with Jennifer. And Jennifer begins to resent the role she has been forced to play. She hates having to be the only one to make social arrangements. She loses her respect for Jason. What do you think is likely to happen to their passion for each other?

## A Case Analysis

Let's see what Jason would have to do to convert his character-based love into self-generated love. There are two basic steps he needs to follow. First, Jason must not turn his back on the conflict he has with Jennifer. To do so would be to deny personally valuable data about himself. In brief, Jason's conflict with Jennifer reveals what has not been fully developed in his own personality. Further, avoiding the problem leaves an untreated wound in his relationship.

Jason must actively explore this difficult conflict for what it reveals *about him*. Through self-examination, Jason will eventually see the hole in his development and how he depends on Jennifer to fill it. He acknowledges what this has cost him in terms of his self-respect and the respect of Jennifer.

Second, after accepting the weakness in his personality, Jason must now embark on the difficult task of developing his own internal resources. He must learn the specific skills of taking the social initiative, making plans, and finding out what his friends enjoy doing. This won't be easy. It will be like starting from scratch.

Jason must be guided by what he and Jennifer stand to gain from his efforts. Jason's immediate goal is to become self-reliant. His long-term goal is to become more self-respecting in relation to Jennifer. Interestingly, Jason's efforts will earn him more than the development of a valuable personality trait. He will acquire greater emotional maturity, with its accompanying feelings of self-respect. Moreover, he will enjoy greater respect from Jennifer. Imagine how Jennifer's feelings for Jason will improve as she observes his efforts to bring about a positive change in himself. The love that was lost will be restored. It will be self-generated.

### Language Metaphor

Picture yourself growing up in a family where your parents spoke to you in two languages, Spanish and English. As a small child you would have easily learned both of these languages as they were spoken to you. The reason for this is that as small children, our brains are predisposed to acquire language rapidly. All we need is the right language stimulation, someone to speak to us.

The same is true for self-generated love. All we need is the right emotional stimulation. Early learning is a distinct advantage. Now picture yourself growing up in an ideal family where your parents cared for you with the kind of love and respect that match your individual needs. As a result, you emerge as an adult with love and respect for yourself.

What does an ideal parent actually do that enables the child to grow up with self-respect? Essentially, good parents do three basic things well: They identify, legitimatize, and help represent their children's needs. When this is done consistently, children learn to trust and respect themselves and other people.

## Personal Exercise

Think back to the time when you were first dating your current partner. What were the personality qualities you fell in love with? Why were you drawn to these qualities? Make a list of them. Now, ask yourself, have these traits changed? Or has your view of these traits changed? If your answer is yes to either of these questions, how has your relationship been affected?

Now, think about how you might improve your relationship by developing your skills at self-generating love. Conceptually, this is simple, but applying it can be challenging. To start, identify one of your needs (maybe one that won't pose as much initial difficulty), make it legitimate, and then represent it to your partner.

# Chapter Four
# The Basics of Intimacy

It's Saturday night, and it's Vicki's turn to clean up after dinner. She looks at her husband, Tom, who's sitting in front of the television, and fantasizes about the two of them slipping off to enjoy champagne before a warm fire. She pictures the two of them snuggling together and kissing tenderly, each absorbed in the other. But Vicki is afraid to ask Tom, knowing how badly he wants to watch the championship boxing match tonight.

Do you identify with Vicki or Tom? Are you afraid to ask for what you want? What are the benefits and risks? And what happens when we don't ask for what we want? Unfortunately, asking involves risk, and risking evokes fear. Can we learn to make friends with fear and become more intimate?

## Intimacy Is Unique and Difficult

The intimate relationship is the most unique relationship. It is in a league of its own, not to be compared to any other relationship. Intimacy is unique because it reveals us and renders us vulnerable. It opens us up like a surgeon's scalpel, exposing the deeper and hidden parts of our personalities. It forces our deepest needs and emotions to the surface. It creates a special circumstance in which we cannot escape from ourselves. Sooner or later our flaws, foibles, and imperfections become glaringly obvious to ourselves and to our partners. There are more ways than one to be naked. In short, we become transparent.

Intimacy is also difficult. It is difficult because it is painful. It makes us look at aspects of our personalities we may not want to face. Remember, our partners acquire a personal knowledge of us, making it possible for them to see us as nobody else does. They are in a unique position to use this knowledge to point out our weakest qualities. They reveal our weaknesses in a variety of ways, and we are forced to deal with them, one way or another.

Intimacy is difficult because we not only have to tolerate what our partners see in us, but we must also take responsibility for what intimacy reveals. We have an exposed and untreated emotional wound. For example, suppose your wife confronts you about not doing enough work around the house. And you know she's right. After all, she knows your track record all too well because she has lived with you under the same roof for a long time.

Now here's the dilemma. You have the choice whether to face what she reveals about you. Obviously, this is difficult. If you go ahead and accept what she saying about you (you're not contributing your fair share), you may have to admit your wrongdoing and do more work around the house. Or should you defend yourself by ignoring her or counterattacking? The problem intensifies.

## Managing What Is Revealed

Intimacy is unique and difficult because it creates conflict and intense feelings. In fact, it is the very nature of intimacy to create these difficult encounters between partners. These intense feelings are the result of having our negative qualities revealed. Unfortunately, these intimate conflicts pose enormous obstacles for most of us.

Fear is intimacy's greatest nemesis. Simple advice like, "We must communicate better," misses the point. Underneath our "lack of communication" lurk the fears that breed poor need management. As we struggle to overcome our fears of being open and vulnerable, the path is laid for effective need management, resulting in better communication. Let's develop these points further, but this time on a more personal basis.

Go back and analyze the worst fight you've had with your partner. Who won? Were there really any winners? Actually, we think both of you had an opportunity to gain. Here's how. Look at your most intense feelings. What can they teach you? What would you have to do to manage these feelings effectively? More specifically, *what would you have to change about yourself in order to more effectively manage the feelings your partner reveals about you?* By analyzing your argument, you create an opportunity to discover more about yourself and the feelings your mate stirs within you. To help you with this, let's re-examine how we might analyze a conflict using our ongoing example of Vicki and Tom.

Remember, Vicki wanted romance but was afraid to ask Tom. What can Vicki's fear of risking teach her about herself? This is a critical question Vicki needs to answer. Because her fears prevent her from managing her needs, Vicki must now deal with feelings of frustration and hurt. She may even blame Tom for these feelings.

Making matters worse, she might also create a story about Tom as unromantic, self-centered, and uncaring. And she may even relate to Tom on the same basis. Vicki's storytelling actually avoids the difficult changes she must make in herself. It is the direct result of poor need management and arouses intense negative feelings toward herself and Tom. These feelings are then experienced as diminished love of herself and contempt for her partner.

Consider some other options Vicki has for managing her needs. For instance, Vicki could manage her needs and feelings by identifying and legitimatizing them ("I want to be romantic, and this is perfectly understandable"). This process will also reveal Vicki's fears ("I am afraid Tom will get upset with me").

In order for Vicki to effectively represent her needs, she must first manage her fears and then express them to Tom ("I really want to be romantic with you, but I'm afraid you'll be upset with me"). If this is too frightening for Vicki, she could make a positive reference to the last time she and Tom were romantic. For example, she might say, "Remember, the last time we sat in front of the fire holding hands? I felt very close to you." This approach represents Vicki's needs, but does so in a less threatening manner. It has the additional advantage of conveying a respectful compliment to Tom.

As difficult as this might seem, if Vicki were to follow one of these options, she would like herself more in relation to Tom. It would eliminate her negative story about Tom. And as a consequence, she would like Tom more too. This is self-generated love. Even if Tom were to tell Vicki "No," she could still feel good about herself for having represented her needs in a direct and responsible way. In this manner, Vicki builds self-respect independent of Tom's response to her request. She wins regardless.

## The Fear of Intimacy

Intimacy is a frightening experience. The fear aroused by intimacy is unlike any other type of fear. It is more complicated. It reveals personal vulnerabilities. Figuratively, it is like standing naked in front of your partner and feeling the tensions of embarrassment and vulnerability. Every physical shortcoming is open for viewing. During the intimate moment, we are left unprotected. A moment passes during which there is no certainty; we teeter on a precipice with nothing to cling to. We are completely revealed.

Remember those difficult moments when thoughts like these burned through you: *Do you really love me? Will you marry me? Will my needs or desires matter? Will you make love with me? Will my sexual performance disappoint you?* These are personally revealing moments. Also, each of these moments is pregnant with the tension of uncertainty. Intimacy requires that we manage this double-layered vulnerability. On the one hand, we face the dangers of exposing our needs and having them rejected. On the other hand, we may achieve acceptance and fulfillment if our needs are met.

What do you do at these critical moments when personal vulnerabilities are revealed and outcomes are uncertain? Do you usually play it safe? Or do you take risks? If you take risks, what kind of risks are you most likely to take? How do you feel after you've risked? And if you don't take risks, what becomes of your unmanaged needs and the feelings associated with them? How you answer these questions gives you an opportunity for greater self-understanding and self-management.

# Our Needs Define Us

What is a need? A need is a desire, want, or wish. It is a will to action. Needs are self-charged. They motivate our behavior, pushing and pulling us in a particular direction. In the case of Vicki and Tom, what is wanted? The need is Vicki's desire to be romantic with her husband.

What we need helps define who we are. Our needs also organize and direct our behavior. Sometimes our needs are shallow and fleeting, and their impact on our choices is minimal. At other times, our needs are deep and stable and have enormous impact on our decisions, relationships, and lives. Knowing what we need, why we need it, and how to get what we need is vital to our self-understanding and self-respect. This means it is also vital for the intimate relationship.

## Our History of Needs

There is a traceable history to what we need. This is especially true when it comes to our intimate wants. Early family experiences set a standard against which we compare all future intimate relationships. We try to recreate the positive parts of our past in the present moments of our current relationships. It is as though our needs have been transplanted from an old garden into the soil of a new garden. Will my needs flourish or wither in the new garden? Will my needs be met, rejected, or changed into a form beyond my recognition?

Let's examine this last point with a personal example. One of the authors grew up in a home in which his parents supported his sense of humor. He felt his parents' love and approval when they acknowledged his efforts to be funny. Their approval made him feel valued and esteemed. Now in his marriage, he needs his wife to respond in the same way. When he tries to be funny, he expects her to laugh as a sign of his value to her. Past needs dictate present needs. *Old needs never die.*

In your intimate relationship, what are your needs, and how do they influence your behavior? Can you trace your needs to your early family experiences? What do you find? How does your past affect what you need now? What do these insights tell you about yourself and how you relate to your partner?

## I Fear What I Need

Intimate needs arouse intense feelings. Fear is chief among them. This is especially true when we communicate our needs to our partners. After all, our partners may reject us. Even the anticipation of rejection produces fear. Sometimes it can be so intense that we don't do or say anything. In this sense, we cannot need without experiencing some level of fear. The next question is, how do we manage our fears?

Back to Vicki and Tom. It's Vicki's turn to do the dishes, and while standing at the sink, she fantasizes about having a romantic evening with Tom. She would like to act on her fantasy, but the thought of asking Tom frightens her. Vicki even feels anger as she anticipates Tom's rejection. What should Vicki do to manage her needs and fears?

## Managing Needs and Fears

On the surface, Vicki needs to fulfill her fantasy. She needs a fire, champagne, and snuggling with Tom. On a deeper level, she needs emotional closeness with her husband. The demands of her management position at the office have left her exhausted and depleted. Vicki's need for romance helps define her. Nothing would please her more than to have Tom read her mind and fulfill her desires without the risk of asking. Unfortunately, Vicki recognizes that this is just wishful thinking.

Tom's needs seem to be at odds with Vicki's. On the surface, Tom wants the thrill of watching an exciting sports event. On a deeper level, Tom needs to disengage from the stresses of his hectic work schedule. He also needs Vicki to support his interest in unwinding in front of the television. So, Vicki needs closeness, and Tom needs relief from stress. How can they resolve their differences? How can each of them manage their needs? We will come back to this example later.

## Making Friends with Fear

Managing what we need requires that we *make friends with fear*. This means that we try to bring more of ourselves into the intimate relationship in spite of the dangers. Simply put, we learn to ask for what we need or want, especially for the personal things that mean the most to us. Unfortunately, asking for what we need will arouse our fears of embarrassment, hurt, and rejection. How do we make friends with fear?

Fortunately, psychologists have found that *knowledge* coupled with *exposure* to fear decreases fear. The knowledge part of this plan requires that we change the harmful beliefs associated with our needs.

## Knowledge

Let's illustrate these points with our working example of Vicki and Tom. Vicki wants to be romantic; however, she fears Tom will refuse her. Her feelings are harmful because they paralyze her from taking action. And because she's not actively managing her need, Vicki sets herself up to blame Tom or even herself. Her need is coupled with the fear that Tom will reject her. This type of thinking undermines effective need management. If we could coach Vicki, we would suggest that she modify her thinking to emphasize the rewards of effective need management.

The model we advocate teaches us to prioritize the management of our needs as being more important than simply gratifying them. By focusing on the benefits of effective need management, Vicki can learn how to better handle her fears. This means learning what she can gain simply by managing her needs without necessarily gratifying them. To exclusively focus on need gratification, and the possibility that Tom may frustrate or reject her, only intensifies Vicki's fears.

For example, Vicki might now think from her new vantage point, "If I risk, I might get exactly what I need. If Tom chooses to watch the boxing match, it does not mean that he will continue to refuse me when the event is over. I just need to relax and manage my feelings." Specifically, Vicki needs to identify and legitimatize her needs. This involves the difficult process of reframing her negative thinking and focusing on the positive aspects of her romantic needs. Vicki might say, "I feel close to you when we share time by the fire." By representing her need to Tom in a way that demonstrates respect for him, Vicki can increase her self-esteem and lessen her fears.

Vicki should focus upon what *she does* rather than on how Tom responds. By focusing on herself and what she can do to manage her needs, she can minimize her fears. This is not easy. Most of us evaluate our success on whether or not our needs are gratified. Vicki should avoid this common pitfall by concentrating on what she can control the most—herself. Her goal is to effectively manage her needs. This allows her to like who she is in relation to Tom.

## Exposure

Exposure involves facing our fears again and again—going into the lion's den. Repeated exposure decreases fear. This would be like watching the same frightening movie over and over again until the film no longer arouses any fear.

What would motivate us to face our fears? The answer is knowledge. Knowledge is a powerful motivator. We are empowered by the knowledge that the personal gains from facing our fears, and then the act of risking, outweigh the dangers of these risks and the alternative—doing nothing. Knowledge is not sufficient, however. We must also take action by repeatedly facing our fears.

In the example of Vicki and Tom, Vicki not only needs to reframe her fears (knowledge); she must also take corrective action by facing her fears. She can do this by asking for what she wants again and again (exposure). For instance, Vicki must regularly practice going into the lion's den. She might say to Tom, "It would mean a lot to me if we could snuggle tonight." Every time Vicki asks for what she needs, it helps reduce her fears. Effective need management is a learned skill. It requires practice.

## Redoing the History

When we look back, we often fault ourselves for not expressing our needs in the critical moment. We reflect on what we could have said to our partners, but didn't. However, the good news is that need management is often much more doable after the fact. Once "cooler heads" prevail, we can create an opportunity to return to our partners and express our previously unmanaged need and the fear associated with it. At this point, the need is less intense and therefore easier to manage.

By redoing our personal need history in this fashion, we accomplish three things: First, we practice the skills of need identification, legitimization, and representation. Second, exposure decreases the intensity of our deepest fears. Third, we increase the probability of effectively managing our needs in the future.

Now let's see how you might apply the ideas of knowledge, exposure, and redoing the history to your own relationship. Sit down and express one of your needs to your partner. Try to describe the fears that are connected to your needs. Believe us, they are always there. Remember, the primary goal is not necessarily getting what you need, but showing respect for yourself by effectively *representing* your need. Keep in mind, too, that the fulfillment of improved self-respect will not come easily. Usually, the things that have the greatest value are not easily obtained.

Let's explain this point. We need to face our fears because it makes us like ourselves more. Facing our fears is a type of risking that builds our self-esteem. How does this happen? We like ourselves more because we are in better balance. There is greater harmony between what we need and what we do; we are more integrated. We like ourselves more because we have accomplished something that is difficult and courageous.

Further, facing our fears helps define us. We build a stronger sense of who we are by virtue of the risks we take to manage our needs. Again, it's not easy. But the reward is feeling good about who you are and how you affirm yourself in an intimate relationship.

## The Psychology of Risking

**Risk 1:** Bryan bursts into his wife's office with a dozen red roses on Valentine's Day and loudly proclaims in front of everyone, "I love you, Rosa!"

**Risk 2:** In spite of her husband's recent unemployment, Brittany nervously announces, "I'm pregnant."

**Risk 3:** Heartbroken by her husband's affair, Sue searches her soul, struggles, and declares, "I'm devastated, but I'm willing to stay if you'll join me in marriage counseling."

These are all examples of well-managed risks. In each case, need management involves both personal vulnerability and a potential gain for the risk-taker. The dangers include the potential for embarrassment and rejection. But the potential benefits are enormous. The payoffs are increased self-respect, improved intimacy, and love for our partners. T. S. Eliot wrote, "Only those who will risk going too far can possibly find out how far one can go."

### Risking Intimately

An intimate risk is sharing a personal need that places us in a vulnerable position. If we don't feel some degree of vulnerability and the fear that goes with it, then we are not connecting fully with ourselves. This means we will not make a good intimate connection with our partners. And without this form of "risk-talk," intimacy ultimately dies. In brief, intimacy with our partner first requires intimacy with ourselves.

In the first example above, when Bryan proclaims his love for Rosa, he risks looking odd or foolish. Yet his risking potentially enhances his relationship. When you read what Bryan did, how did you feel? It wouldn't be surprising if you felt a little embarrassment, shame, and admiration for Bryan all rolled into one. Bryan's assertion took courage. He was revealed for the love he felt for Rosa. However, he was vulnerable in that he might have embarrassed himself or Rosa. Similarly, Brittany and Sue took risks by declaring their difficult decisions. Had they not taken these risks, intimacy would have suffered. Risk-taking is vital. Without taking risks, our needs will be inadequately managed. Risking is the life-blood of effective need management and therefore is essential to intimacy.

## I Risk, Therefore I Am

The benefits of intimate risk-taking are dramatic. Our partners will find it hard to love someone they don't fully know. The more our partners know us, the more deeply they can connect with us. If we don't risk revealing what is inside us, then we can't be loved for who we really are. Ironically, this is not easy, because taking risks places us in a position of potentially losing the affection of our loved ones. However, we win affection and respect when we wisely take the risks that let our partners know more about us.

Another benefit of risk-taking is self-development. Sharing our needs and the feelings connected to them allows us to know and to respect ourselves. Who we are comes into sharper focus. And the result is always the same: *If I like who I am when I am with you, then I like you too.* Self-development translates into a healthier relationship.

How do you feel after you have risked making more of yourself known to your partner? For example, imagine you've just had a fight. Now picture how you might respond to your partner. "I really need to talk to you about our argument last night. I was too defensive. I said things I didn't mean. I was wrong."

Consider what this sort of risk-talk really entails. We must identify what we need, legitimatize our needs, and then represent them in a way that balances self and partner respect. Your thoughts are organized, your feelings have been expressed, and you have initiated a positive action in support of yourself and your relationship.

Can you recall a time when you did something like this? If so, how did you feel? This is exactly the kind of situation in which we feel whole and complete. Our thoughts, feelings, and actions are integrated. We are effectively managing ourselves, and as a result we love ourselves *and our* partners!

This might be a good time to pause for a moment and examine your risk-taking skills. We have designed a short quiz to give you a better idea of your strengths and weaknesses in this area.

## Risk for Intimacy — Quiz

**Money Issues**

1. Can you ask for money from your partner?
2. Can you ask for money you've lent to be returned?
3. Can you spend money on yourself?
4. Do you contribute equally in issues over money?
5. Do you attempt to control or give up control over money issues?

**Sex Issues**

1. Can you ask your partner to make love to you?
2. Can you ask your partner for novel forms of sex?
3. Can you turn down your partner's request for sex?
4. Can you tell your partner what you need during sex?

### Feeling Issues

1. Can you tell your partner that you love him/her?

2. Can you acknowledge to your partner the specific ways in which you feel loved by him/her?

3. Can you express anger, hurt, fear, and sadness to your partner?

4. Can you express shame and embarrassment to your partner?

5. Can you tell your partner what he/she does that pleases you?

6. Can you express your sense of humor?

7. Can you enjoy your partner's efforts at humor?

### Family Issues

1. Can you discuss differences in child-rearing with your partner?

2. Can you tell your partner your true feelings about your in-laws?

3. Can you turn down a family request to do what you would like?

4. Can you ask your family to comply with your own plans?

5. Can you problem solve with family members?

Obviously, there are no right or wrong answers to the quiz you've just taken. However, your self-reflections will point out areas where your risk-taking may need some fine-tuning. Remember, the quality of your intimacy will be strongly influenced by your capacity for risking.

# Strategies for Risk-Taking

We hope this quiz has given you a clearer sense of your risk-taking abilities. Keep in mind that risking is like any learned skill—it takes time to develop. Now, take a look at the ideas below to see if you can apply them to help you become a better risk-taker. You have probably noticed that the ideas presented to this point have been fairly abstract. Now let's take an opportunity to offer some practical and time-tested suggestions on risk-taking as it applies to intimacy. Consider the following:

1.  We need to understand that there is no way to avoid risking. In the long run, playing it safe—or worse, doing nothing—is the greatest risk. It can even be destructive. Everything we do or don't do has consequences. The point is to know how to manage our needs as well as the risks that accompany them.

2.  Since everything we do involves risking of some kind, our only viable option is to identify, legitimatize, and represent our needs. Remember, effective need management promotes self and partner respect. The best risk-taking decisions are those that lead us to respect ourselves and our partners.

3.  It is important for us to place greater emphasis upon the changes that occur to our character when we risk, instead of focusing on the outcomes. In other words, it is better to develop self-respect than to get our partners to gratify our needs. By practicing this value, we make the health of the relationship more important than the gratification of our immediate personal needs.

4.  It is also important to distinguish healthy from non-healthy risk-taking. A healthy risk is a well-managed risk. A healthy risk means that we follow the principles of effective need management. It often requires us to be thoughtful and deliberate. We don't just let our needs "out of the bag." We have to look within ourselves and effectively manage our needs. Remember, we also have to be aware of our partners' needs and take those into consideration when we open up and risk.

5. Remember that risking gets easier the more we do it. Practice makes us better when it comes to risk-taking in intimacy. This is especially true in managing our fears.

6. Expect a reaction. Risking is likely to create a reaction from our partners. Good risk-taking always involves balancing self and partner respect. Be willing to listen and respect your partner's position. Remember, our highest priority is effective need management and not need gratification.

7. Manage your emotions. Intense emotions often derail our best efforts. Wait until you calm down. Timing can be a crucial part of effective need management. It's another means by which you can show respect for your partner and yourself. You want all your wits about you! If your emotions are too intense, then it will be harder to work with your partner. Remember, the stronger your emotions, the more actively they must be managed.

## The Safety in Risking

Ironically, emotional safety and security come from our ability to take risks. Here's how this works. Shakespeare said, "To thine own self be true and thou canst not be false to any man." By our translation, being "true" to ourselves requires that we take risks by managing our needs. This means we identify, legitimatize, and represent our needs. Our failure to assume these risks results in loss of identity. But calculated risk-taking defines our unique qualities as individuals. Further, to the extent we make known who we are by taking risks, we will be "true" to ourselves and our partners. And therein lies the greatest safety.

## Need Management and Intimacy

Managing what we need and the feelings associated with our needs is crucial to intimacy. Why? If we know what we want and manage it effectively, we not only value ourselves, but our partners as well. *Remember, we can be no more intimate with our partners than we are intimate with ourselves.* Identifying our needs promotes self-definition. And managing what we want creates self-respect. In truth, the love we have for our partners is a reflection of how well we know and manage ourselves. Does this sound strange to you? Yet, how can we love our partners if we don't like who we are when we are with them?

## Personal Exercise

Becoming a good need manager takes time, effort, and a lot of practice. Keep this in mind while you try an exercise to strengthen your need management skills. Start by identifying a personal need. Make it simple, one that's not too difficult to manage.

Now, without doing or saying anything to your partner, imagine going through each of the steps of good need management. Allow yourself to visualize everything you'd have to do to complete each step of the model. Feel yourself overcoming your fear as you identify your need. You are making friends with fear. Go out of your way to make your need legitimate. Praise yourself for having the need. Now, imagine yourself expressing your need to your partner. You are going into the lion's den and are taking a well-managed risk.

As you move through the steps of effective need representation, picture yourself balancing self and partner respect. Express your need in a way that captures the deepest feelings connected to your need. Feeling the deeper connection you now have with yourself, you anticipate the bond you will have with your partner. Keep in mind, your connection to your partner can be no better than your connection to yourself. Can you feel the intimacy you're creating? If not, you may wish to review this chapter before proceeding.

# Chapter Five
# Overcoming Emotional Wounds

Everybody has emotional wounds. Escaping childhood without some degree of emotional injury is impossible. We are all victims of incomplete parenting. To heal our wounds and further our emotional development, we must learn to parent ourselves, or we'll bring our emotional injuries into our current intimate relationships. We can be no more intimate with our partners than we are resolved of the past and the hold it has on us.

## Vignette

Diana felt an unexplained and growing rift with her husband, Justin. The conflict began when the two of them were discussing the renovation of their kitchen. In what seemed to Diana like a radical change of character, Justin fell in love with some very expensive architectural plans. He began to plead for them like a hungry little boy in a candy shop.

Normally, Diana would do just about anything to make Justin happy, but this triggered something unsettling in her that was hard to understand. When Justin tried to convince Diana how beautiful their new kitchen would be, she felt herself becoming withdrawn and quietly angry. Justin continued to make an emotional pitch for the new plans, but his efforts were met with a growing wall of resistance. Finally, at her wits' end, Diana angrily demanded, "I don't want to talk about this."

The argument upset Diana for several weeks until she realized the source of her feelings. She had been reliving a childhood experience, and the words "unnecessary extravagance" popped into her mind. At this point, Diana remembered a heart-wrenching experience. When she was ten years old, her mother had spent a lot of money on a new dress for her to wear to a friend's birthday party. She recalled how happy her mother had been in providing it for her, almost as happy as she herself had been.

But that evening when her father returned home from work, she overheard the two of them arguing over the money her mother had spent on the dress. She remembered the harsh tones in her father's voice and the tearful but inadequate defense her mother made on her behalf. She remembered how her father would frequently refer to the dress as an "unnecessary extravagance." She even harbored deep feelings of self-blame for causing her mother so much suffering. From that time on, Diana felt conflicted about money spent on anything that could be considered unnecessary or extravagant.

## Past Relationship: Our Parents

There are two essential relationships: the one we had with our parents (past), and the one we have with our mates (present). All other relationships pale by comparison. No other relationships carry the same weight. The relationship we had with our parents was formative in that we became who we are under their care and guidance. We had our first and most significant experiences with them. Under their care, we learned the basics: how to walk, talk, relate to others, value ourselves, and develop many of our current personality traits. Quite literally, the quality of our parents' care shaped who we are.

Unfortunately, their care was imperfect. As a result, we also learned traits that undermine our future relationships. Look at a personal example of one of the authors. In his words:

"My father was one of twelve children raised on a small farm in Northern Utah. As you might imagine, parental attention was spread thin. Out of necessity, he learned to rely upon himself. At seventeen, my father left his home on a single-speed bicycle and pedaled to San Francisco in search of a job with $7.50 in his pocket.

"Naturally, my father's self-reliance was a big part of how he parented me. I grew up valuing independence and self-sufficiency. These are admirable traits that ought to be a part of anyone's character. However, in an intimate relationship these qualities need to be balanced by cooperation and teamwork. I get into trouble if my independence prevails when teamwork is called for. Just ask my wife!"

## Present Relationship: Our Partners

Our present partners reveal who we are. It is the next intimacy. This relationship is essential because it makes known what was and was not developed in our formative relationship with our parents.

No one knows us like our intimate partners. There is no place to hide. Intimacy leaves us exposed. It reveals all of our imperfections, flaws, and foibles. It is the most intense and complex relationship; no other relationship creates deeper conflict. We are exposed for who we are. However, because of intimacy's unique ability to reveal us, we are in the position to use this information for personal growth.

What do our partners reveal about us? They reveal many things, but most importantly, *they reveal our incomplete emotional development.* In broad terms, this includes our fears about being loved and getting our needs met. For example, take a moment and refer to our couple. What do you think Justin revealed about Diana? Justin's desire for an expensive new kitchen triggered Diana's conflict overspending money. Diana was afraid that spending money for the kitchen was too extravagant. Her fear brought up old memories from her past. In a nutshell, Justin had aroused Diana's insecurity. This is what intimacy does. It aggressively finds and reveals our weaknesses. It shines a glaring light on our incomplete development.

## Crossing the Bridge from Past to Present

The early relationship with our parents greatly influences our relationships with our intimate partners. What we failed to develop in childhood comes screaming back to haunt us in our present relationships. For example, if we didn't develop an adequate sense of trust during childhood, then we may be unable to fully accept or enjoy our partners' love in the present. We are left open and vulnerable to any signs of our partners' lack of caring or rejection. We are also more prone to overreact by blaming our partners, becoming hurt or angry, or running away.

This process moves in two ways across the bridge connecting the present with the past. The emotional problems with our partners can open up old wounds from our past. For instance, Justin's desire to remodel the kitchen aroused Diana's old emotional issues about spending money. And our past also affects how we relate to our partners in the present. Diana's early family conflicts set her up to be reactive to her husband's "extravagant" spending. In short, the past affects the present, and the present reactivates the past.

## Emotional Wounds

Remember, no one escapes childhood without emotional damage. We are all victims of imperfect parenting; therefore, we are all psychologically injured. What are emotional wounds, and what becomes of them?

Emotional wounds are painful and unresolved childhood experiences. These injuries occur in past relationships and leap forward in time to negatively impact our current relationships. For example, Diana's pain over the dress issue (past) makes her vulnerable to her husband's desire for an expensive new kitchen (present). Diana's emotional wound from her past reappeared in her present relationship with Justin. Diana is experiencing the damage of her past.

How do our unhealed emotional wounds affect our current intimate relationships? There are several ways this can happen. First, unhealed emotional wounds make us more vulnerable to current stress. Picture a boxer who has just sustained four sharp blows to his head. He is still standing, but with the fifth punch he drops to the mat even though the last blow was the weakest. The initial punches left him in a vulnerable state. This is also true for emotional injuries. Imagine a young child whose parents divorced. As an adult, she is very sensitive to rejection and loss.

Second, old and unhealed wounds leave us sensitive to new injury. We are afraid of being hurt again. To protect ourselves from further hurt, we become defensive and create stories about ourselves and our partners. For example, we may think of ourselves as "unlovable" or that our partners are "selfish and uncaring." We then believe these stories about ourselves and our partners and act as if they were true. In other words, we act like we are unloved and expect our partners to show little or no affection. The end result is that we get hurt again.

Third, unresolved wounds make us overreact even to the point of manufacturing problems that don't exist. We are quick to color our partners' behaviors in a negative way. For example, many people complain that their partners are "controlling" them. Actually, their partners may simply want something that means a great deal to them, and they express these wants in strong ways. They may not intend to control.

### A Case Example

We can get a different look at the effects of the past by examining a typical fight between a husband and wife. Their conflict is over child discipline. She sees him as too rigid and strict. He sees her as too "wishy-washy." And so the fight continues. He sees it one way, she sees it another. His past upbringing influences his thinking about how the children should be raised. Her past also influences how she thinks children ought to behave. The past is formative.

Their early experiences have shaped their current thinking. Now, each partner is stuck. When this occurs, it points out the grip the past can have upon us and the emotional damage that can result.

## The Importance of Past Relationships

When we survey the damage of our past, we are taking a very close look at our earliest relationships. The way our parents related to us formed who we are and how we fit into the world. We learned what to expect and value in ourselves and our relationships.

Our relationship with our parents is formative. They shape our development. In a healthy family, parents support and nurture their children. Parents observe the unfolding characteristics of their children and provide vital emotional support that furthers the children's growth. Young children are dependent on this emotional support.

Imagine a six-year-old girl picking up a crayon and drawing a picture that shows artistic promise. When her parents encourage her (emotional support), she begins to see herself in the same positive way they see her. Her specific needs for recognition and praise are met. By this means, her parents influence the concept she has of herself. In other words, a young child cannot manufacture self-esteem completely on his or her own. It has to be supplied by those obligated to care for the child.

## Imperfect Parents

We know perfect parents do not exist. None of us escapes childhood without suffering some emotional scars. This leaves each of us with a very important job—*to complete our own parenting and continue the business of growing up.* Now as adults, we must survey, repair, and complete the development begun in our childhood. If we don't rise to this challenge, we suffer, and so do our intimate partners who are left with the burden of our incomplete development. Our partners are stuck living with our deficiencies, and we are stuck living with theirs. Wounded partners live with a time bomb that can explode at any moment.

## Imperfect Childhood

There is no such thing as a perfect childhood. Some of us by sheer chance had it better than others. And some of us were very unfortunate when it came to getting good parenting. Consider what happens when the necessary parental support for our development is incomplete, neglectful, or abusive. How are we affected? When child care is defective, development goes off track. We don't develop to our fullest potential. What would happen to a child born with a talent for music if no one took the time to nurture the child's abilities? The child's talents would wither away.

Let's look at these ideas with a simple example. Picture the seed of a plant before it germinates. Its genes are dormant, waiting to grow, to realize their potential. But in order to grow, the seed must have the right amount of sunlight, water, and soil. If any of these vital supplies is defective or missing, it will not grow in the same way. In the wrong environment, the seed fails to develop its potential. In the right environment, the seed will flourish.

Personalize this point by putting yourself under the microscope. What was missing in your relationship with your parents? If your care was less than ideal, how were you affected? Later, we'll test you on these points with a quiz. Remember that this mental exercise is not intended to blame our parents, but to learn to identify and manage our needs.

## Unmet Needs

When a child's emotional needs are not met, do they simply disappear? Does the child outgrow them like a toy that becomes too juvenile? Our emotional needs are not outgrown; they follow us everywhere. In particular, we bring our unmet needs into the next stages of development and into the next round of relationships. Noted family therapists Ivan Boszormenyi-Nagy and Barbara

Krasner state that when a child's emotional needs go unmet, they reappear in later relationships in ways that are often destructive.

Imagine a young child who needs her father's approval. She needs to know her father thinks of her as valuable and capable. Unfortunately, her needs go largely unmet. As she grows into adolescence, you can probably guess what happens. She is vulnerable to the flirtations and immature affections of her male friends, particularly the older ones. She idealizes these friends. They appear to be the answer to her dreams of being loved and cherished. She finds herself doing things out of a need for attention that she later regrets. Her adolescent misadventures into romance are primarily intended to fill the emotional needs that were not met in her relationship with her father.

## Surveying the Damage of the Past

Take a moment to survey the damage of your own past. To do this, ask yourself what you needed from your parents. Keep in mind we are not referring to material things. We are talking about emotional supplies that bring about individual growth and development, such as love, trust, and understanding.

For example, when we ask our clients what they needed from their parents, they often respond by saying, "more love," "more time," "more understanding," "more protection," and "more safety." Interestingly, some have even said, "more discipline." Each of these emotional supplies is intended to target or identify specific developmental needs and nurture their growth. Of course, what we needed from our parents changed from one developmental period to the next. But most of us needed the same essential emotional supplies regardless of our stage of development or our individual needs.

If you have children, there is a quick way to assess the emotional supplies you needed from your own parents. Ask yourself what you feel you need to provide for your children. We tend to give our children what we did not get from our own parents. One of the authors never heard the words "I love you" from his father. Now he makes sure his children hear these words often.

We have devised a brief quiz that will help you evaluate the type and amount of emotional support you got or didn't get from your parents. Rate yourself on each of the ten areas below by indicating the number that comes closest to your experience.

**Very Little-----Moderate-----Excessive**

**1---2---3---4---5---6---7---8---9---10**

1. Trust _____
2. Protection/Safety _____
3. Discipline _____
4. Praise/Rewards _____
5. Understanding _____
6. Guidance _____
7. Encouragement _____
8. Fun/Recreation _____
9. Respect _____
10. Communication _____

*Survey Results and Analysis*

To find your score and understand what it means, add your ratings for each category. Then divide your total score by ten (the number of categories) and compare this number to the scale at the top of the quiz. The best scores are those that fall in the mid-range, that is, scores from 4 to 7. Extreme scores may indicate that parental support was either "under-provided" or "over-provided." You might ask, how can a parent provide too much guidance? Remember, if a parent offers too much guidance, the child may feel inadequate. Emotional support must strike a balance between too little parenting and too much parenting.

If you scored in the mid-range, this suggests that most of the time your parents provided "reasonable or optimal" levels of support. Extreme scores (1, 2, 3, and 8, 9, 10) imply that the influence your parents had may not have been consistent with your developmental or emotional needs.

Your quiz results can be very revealing if you consider them carefully. For instance, one client rated a high score on Encouragement (8), but gave low ratings on Guidance and Discipline (1, 2 respectively). When he reflected on his ratings, he said, "My parents tried to encourage me by saying I could do or be anything I wanted in life, but without their strong guidance and discipline, their encouragement fell flat."

It is very important to understand that this exercise and the ideas related to it are not intended to blame our parents! They too were victims of imperfect parenting. Further, blaming keeps us locked in a cycle of victimization. This is not to excuse the actions of some parents who are outright neglectful and abusive. Parents are like potluck dinners; you never know what you are going to get. Regardless of the quality of parenting we received, it is our responsibility to continue our development. Let's stop blaming our parents and learn to parent ourselves.

## Learning from Emotional Wounds

When we bring unhealed emotional wounds into our intimate relationships, we court disaster. And yet the majority of us do just that. We start new relationships without fully understanding and resolving the issues from our previous involvements. We even think our new partners will actually cure us of our old relationship wounds. Or, we naively think we'll never face our old problems again. This kind of thinking sets us up for disappointment, hurt, and even failure.

Instead, we should study our previous relationships and ask some very critical questions: How and why did my relationships end? How did I manage the loss of someone I was close to? How well did I manage my needs in my relationship? What does all this teach me?

With these points in mind, let's turn our attention to some useful strategies for overcoming emotional wounds and increasing intimacy.

## Becoming Your Own Parent

Many of us assume that because we reach the age of adulthood, our development is complete. Nothing could be further from the truth. Childhood and adolescence simply start the process. They don't complete it. *Nowhere is this more evident than in intimacy.* And it is precisely for these reasons that we must continue our development by becoming our own parents.

This is an enormous task. But with effort and practice, we can accomplish a great deal. And our partners will be grateful. To start, ask yourself what you need and may still need from your parents (refer to your survey results). This will require serious reflection. Your partner can be very helpful in this respect. He or she may see things in your personality that you don't.

Let's go back and take the example of Diana a step further. What does she need to do now that she is aware of her old problem with spending money? Or, more broadly, what does she need to do to become her own parent and further her emotional development? Remember, as a child she felt guilty and ashamed over the new dress. She also felt responsible for causing the fight between her parents. For Diana to parent herself, she must *think and act* effectively about her past. She needs to see herself in a new way. This means she must identify her need, make it legitimate, and then learn to represent it. For example, she could say to herself, "The need for nice, new things is perfectly legitimate. And buying nice things is okay when it fits my budget."

It is equally important for Diana to *act* on her new insights. She can do this by talking to both her husband and her parents about the guilt she feels over spending money. Taking action strengthens her new way of thinking. She is representing her need.

## Learning to Think and Act Effectively

Learning to parent ourselves is very challenging. One way to simplify this task is to ask, "What do good parents do to help their children think and act effectively, especially under challenging circumstances?"

Good parents help their children identify their needs and the deepest feelings associated with them. Since our needs define who we are, this has the effect of constructing a positive sense of self in the child. It also decreases the intensity of the child's feelings, making the need more manageable.

Good parenting is effective because it elevates thinking above excessive and disruptive feelings. The strong emotions that often work against effective thinking and problem-solving become more tolerable. The child feels his or her needs are supported and legitimate.

Next, parents gently encourage the child to consider alternative and constructive ways to think about their needs and the best way to manage them. *Guiding without intruding,* parents might ask, "Have you thought of...?" or "What would happen if you were to...?" The benefits of productive thinking and problem-solving are reinforced. By this means, the child's need management skills are shaped.

Now, the child's emotions are in check and his or her ability to think clearly is supported by the parents. The parents serve as guides. They don't take over for the child, nor do they leave the child to stew in his or her own emotions. The role of the parents is to strengthen the child's ability to manage his or her needs. There is no better use of parental authority.

Let's apply these ideas to working with an adult. Go back to our Diana example. Remember, her emotions were strangling her thinking. Her sensitivities about spending money left her feeling ashamed. Now, what would Diana have to do to parent herself?

As an adult, Diana must identify, legitimatize, and represent her need. For example, she might conclude that her need for a new dress (identify) was appropriate (legitimatize). She could also consider how she might have respectfully expressed her need to her parents. Effective need management has enabled Diana to give new meaning to her past as well as *dismantle the hold it has on her*. For example, she might now conclude that it was her parents who had mismanaged their own needs. "Maybe money was tight at the time and Dad was anxious about spending, or maybe Mom and Dad were at odds with each other and the dress became an issue."

With her emotions in check, and by giving a new meaning to her past experience, Diana can loosen the grip her past has on her. She now becomes her own parent. She is learning to manage herself more effectively.

### A Case in Point

Take a look at a common example of how married partners can learn to parent themselves. The husband, Sean, describes his wife, Michelle, as too strict in the way she disciplines their children.

Her methods of child-rearing differ from his. Their conflict sets the stage for his stories about her as too strict and her stories about him as too lenient.

Their conflict is fueled by their different views of each other. Sean sees Michelle as "inflexible and rigid" because she wants to ground their daughter for coming home late. Michelle sees Sean as "lacking backbone" because he wants to warn their daughter instead of punishing her. How should Sean and Michelle deal with their differences? What can they learn about themselves and each other over this hot topic?

Sean and Michelle have a responsibility to explore and understand what their differences reveal about themselves. Let's focus on Sean to see how he might work on his part of the problem. First, he must manage his feelings toward Michelle. One way Sean might do this is to open up and share his feelings about disciplining his daughter. Specifically, after some soul-searching, Sean might reveal to his wife, "I worry that if I am too harsh, she will become angry and reject me." If Sean speaks from his deepest feelings, Michelle will be more likely to open up too, creating the possibility for better communication.

Further, Sean needs to understand how his past family experiences affect his current thinking. Why does he assume his daughter will reject him? Somewhere in Sean's early experience, he learned to connect strong discipline with loss of love. How can Sean undo this connection? By concentrating on what his daughter needs (limits), he is more likely to free himself from the grip of ineffective action.

For instance, if Sean's daughter shows a pattern of returning home late, she would need limits because she is out of control. What Sean's daughter needs is what ought to determine the type of discipline. This tool allows Sean to see himself more objectively. In other words, Sean is learning to stand apart from himself and view his problem differently. He now sees a wider range of options, including the idea that firmness may be necessary.

Sean's self-understanding can lead to changes in his behavior. He is freer to experiment with forms of discipline that are more consistent with his daughter's needs. Sean now must reinforce his new thinking with action. Action strengthens self-understanding and self-management. Now consider one very powerful action tool—reworking our conflicts.

## Reworking Our Conflicts

"Just forget it." "I don't want to talk about it." "Let it alone." "It's over." "It's in the past." These are common expressions used to avoid the discomfort and pain of conflict. It is only natural to want to avoid this pain. *But conflict tends to become worse and reoccur.*

One important way to manage conflict is to change how we think about the problem. Self-examination comes before action and paves the way for improving our behavior. In our example, Sean evaluates his style of discipline by examining his feelings and their origins in his past experience. He looks at how this experience has shaped his feelings and behavior. His new insights then position him to change his method of disciplining his daughter. Sean is prepared to change his behavior.

Equipped with courage gained by his new insight, Sean is now ready to rework his conflict with Michelle. First, he needs to respectfully ask Michelle for her time. Then, Sean needs to engage Michelle in a discussion over discipline. This time their discussion is different. Sean is more vulnerable and insightful. He makes a connection between his past and his present. He is open to change. He asks Michelle to listen and provide emotional support. At this point, Sean is effectively representing his needs. Now his conversation with Michelle flows entirely differently.

Here's how Sean's part of the conversation might go. He could say to Michelle, "I have thought about why I discipline our daughter the way I do. I realize that I have connected firm discipline with rejection and loss. I have done this because of my own early experiences. I'm beginning to understand this has more to do with my past than with what our daughter needs."

Sean can draw strength from knowing that his efforts will bring positive change in his relationship with Michelle even if she is not actively trying to change herself. This happens because Sean and Michelle are part of a "relationship system." When one part of a system changes, then strong influences are brought to bear upon the other part of the system. As Sean assumes a stronger disciplinary role, Michelle will feel less pressure to provide strict discipline to compensate for Sean's leniency. Michelle will have greater freedom to express the "softer side" of herself to her daughter, which was hard for her when she saw Sean as "too lenient." Sean will also find it easier to be firm when he sees Michelle as more flexible and loving. In this way, change in one partner brings change in the other partner.

## Strategies for Overcoming Emotional Wounds

Let's take a closer look at the process of becoming our own parent. When we think and act differently, we are actually engaging in two steps. First, we acknowledge and take responsibility for what our partners are revealing about us. Second, we become effective need managers. With these two points in mind, let's see how our model (Chapter Two) can be useful in generating practical strategies for overcoming emotional wounds. Consider the following steps:

**1. Stop Blaming.** The first step is to stop blaming our partners. Many of us try to avoid our old emotional wounds by blaming our partners. This is counterproductive. Blaming our partners is essentially telling a story about them. She was such a "nag." He was such a "jerk."

*Blaming our partners victimizes us.* We lose our power. The hidden assumption is that our partners have control over what we feel. For example, have you ever blamed a partner for being too controlling? If you have, then how do you feel when you believe your partner has control over you? Actually, your partner can't control you unless you play a passive role. Remember, it is easier to tell a story about our partners than to look at our own unmet needs and learn how to effectively manage them.

**2. Analyze Your Stories.** A story is a negative description of our partners or ourselves. Commonly, it takes the form of blaming. It is not only important to stop blaming our partners, but to examine the stories we tell about them. These stories teach us important information about ourselves. This is one powerful way in which intimacy reveals us.

So, when we accuse our partners of being "controlling," what are we revealing about ourselves? How could our partners be controlling without someone to control? Maybe we are too easily persuaded? Or maybe we are being too passive? If so, we are afraid to assert our needs. Are we afraid of being rejected? Telling a story about our partners temporarily relieves us of the harder task of changing who we are in relation to our partners.

**3. Identify Your Unmet Needs.** The stories we tell about our partners can help us identify our unmet or mismanaged needs. Suppose we create a story about our partner as someone who controls us. What does this tell us about ourselves? Why are we playing a passive role? What is making it difficult for us to identify and express our needs? Do we expect our partners to always gratify our needs? If so, what does this suggest about us? And what usually happens when we leave this task to them? When we fail to represent or effectively manage our needs, we are probably afraid of being rejected by our partners.

What are our unmet needs? Basically, they include the need to be understood, respected, and loved. These needs often go unmet because of our fears of being rejected. In short, telling a story about our partner implies that *they* are ultimately responsible for meeting our needs. In reality, this is next to impossible. First, they cannot read our minds. And second, even if they could read our minds, it is our responsibility to identify, legitimatize, and represent our own needs. Our partners can support us, but not take over this important task.

**4. Learn to Effectively Manage Ourselves.** After identifying our needs, the next question becomes, how can we effectively manage them? Effective self-management means taking action. We must take responsibility for our needs by becoming our own parents—our own heroes! How do we do this? We build the courage to effectively manage our needs by thinking differently about ourselves and our partners.

Then we take action that is consistent with our new thinking. For example, if a husband realizes that he has a growing resentment of his wife for the extra time she's spending at her office, what must he do to manage his needs? Instead of accusing her of selfishness or being uncaring, he might reflect, "How have I managed my needs to be respected and supported for finding time to spend with my wife?"

Specifically, he needs to find a different way to think about his problem, one that will leave him feeling more self-respect. He must also stop resenting his wife (not tell a story about her) and learn to take positive action on his own behalf. Here's what he might do. He could say to his wife, "I know your work at the office is very important to you, and you certainly seem to have a lot of it lately (partner respect). I'd like to plan some time this weekend when you're not quite so busy for just the two of us (self-respect)." By taking actions that respect both himself and his wife, the husband has become his own parent.

**5. Enhance the Relationship.** When we identify and effectively manage our needs, we enhance our relationship. This is how it happens. We can be no more intimate with our partners than we are intimate with ourselves. By identifying our needs and doing what it takes to manage them, we are being intimate with ourselves. We come to know and manage ourselves more effectively. This builds self-respect. And increases in self-respect bring corresponding increases in respect from our partners.

How have you felt about yourself when you have acted courageously and asserted your needs to your partner? How have you felt when your partner has asked you to help meet his or her personal needs? When we stop blaming and identify and manage our needs effectively, good things happen; our relationship improves.

## Personal Exercise

If you haven't had a chance to take the survey, please do so now. Analyze your results. What do you find? If you are like most of us, you will find some damage (low or high scores). Remember, there is no such thing as perfect parents.

The next step takes courage. Go to your partner and explore with him or her how the damage from your past may interfere with your relationship. Be sure to get your partner's point of view. Your partner knows you very well.

The final step is to discuss with your partner how you can best manage this deficit. For example, if you scored low on trust, you may find yourself emotionally constricted and guarded with your partner. Your partner may have some ideas on how this impacts him or her. Your partner will also have some ideas on how you can work to improve. Your partner is your best teacher.

# Chapter Six
# Men vs. Women: The Longest War

The longest war is the war between the sexes. Gender differences both attract and repel us. When we understand, accept, and manage these differences, we can change destructive conflicts into a beneficial union of opposites.

Tracy broke the speed limit driving to her mother's house. She could not have been more excited to tell her mother about her new boyfriend. "Mom, I am so happy about Richard. He is so incredible! I can't wait for you to meet him! He is everything I could love in a man! He is confident and self-assured!" Tracy's mother listened with genuine interest and happiness, but her joy for her daughter was tempered by her own experience with romantic love.

Romance inevitably starts passionately, but soon the passion fades and problems begin. Tracy's mother knows from her own experience that men and women are very different. She knows these differences create tension and conflict. She also knows the love between a man and a woman brings the worst pain and the greatest joy.

## He vs. She—The War Between the Sexes

Tracy's mother is right. Passion fades. And worse, the initial differences that once attracted us soon begin to generate tension and conflict. What are these differences, and how do they cause problems? In the sections to follow, we will examine these differences, how they threaten intimacy, and what we can do about them.

In our relationship workshops, we find it helpful to highlight the differences between men and women. To do this, we use an exercise in which we ask audience members to shout the first thing that comes to mind when they hear the words "masculine" and "feminine." With few exceptions, the audiences come up with roughly the same lists of adjectives. Before you go on, take a moment to consider your own emotional reactions to these words. What are your first thoughts? Now, compare your list with what we usually find:

| Masculine | Feminine |
|---|---|
| 1.  Strong | 1.  Soft |
| 2.  Independent | 2.  Submissive |
| 3.  Aggressive | 3.  Caring |
| 4.  Competitive | 4.  Cooperative |
| 5.  Providers/Bread-Winners | 5.  Family Focused |
| 6.  Competent | 6.  Thoughtful |
| 7.  Non-Emotional | 7.  Emotional |
| 8.  Confident | 8.  Self-Sacrificing |
| 9.  Initiates | 9.  Compliant |
| 10. Sexually Driven | 10. Love Driven |

Were your lists similar to ours? Most likely, you came up with many of the same words. Now, if you look closely at these words you will see that many of them are opposites. In fact, all of these adjectives are stereotypes. It is easy for most of us to over-generalize and inaccurately represent the opposite sex. Unfortunately, we often act as if these stereotypes were true and as a result, engage in unnecessary conflict with our partners.

In the beginning of a relationship, these stereotypes complement one another, especially when partners are attracted to each other. This means when men are viewed as strong and competent, however accurate or inaccurate it may be, it is natural for women to slip into a role complement. They may begin to play soft and compliant. In this "dance," male "strength" is complemented by female "compliance." These roles can be played out in both directions. Her softness helps create his strength; his strength makes possible the expression of her softness. As they play their respective roles, each partner experiences a "romantic high" that is both powerful and addictive.

## An Acceptable Addiction

During romance, male-female differences serve as powerful confirmations of our masculine and feminine sides. The result is a deeply enriching, yet potentially intoxicating and addictive experience none of us forgets. Romance between the sexes is an acceptable addiction. Remember, in our preview Tracy and Richard's differences bring them together. He is confident, while she is nurturing. He is the kind of man she is looking for. She is the kind of woman he is looking for. He is playing masculine; she is playing feminine. Let the games begin!

## Post-Romantic Stress Disorder

You can probably guess what happens next. Differing male and female expectations gradually change into sources of conflict as it becomes increasingly difficult for each partner to continue playing roles that are inaccurate or unrealistic. Think about Tracy and Richard once again. Remember, Tracy saw Richard as strong and confident. But how realistic is it for Richard to be strong, capable and confident all the time? What do you suppose it is like for Tracy to be soft, compliant, and nurturing all the time?

Assuming their relationship develops, there will be numerous occasions during which Richard will find it impossible to be competent and strong. For instance, what happens to Richard's "hero status" when he comes home stressed from a difficult day at work, or worse, if he should lose his job? Likewise, what will happen to Tracy's softness and compliance when she is provoked to anger or circumstances require her to be assertive?

Neither partner can live up to the demands of unrealistic roles. Ironically, the harder each one tries, the more they both are revealed for what they really are—two humans unable to consistently live up to the unrealistic expectations of their gender roles. As each tries and inevitably falls short, problems come into play.

## Mismatched Priorities

There is another important way in which men and women are at odds with each other. Traditionally, men are taught to be breadwinners and career focused. Money, prestige, and power are sometimes male preoccupations. Warren Farrell, a prominent writer in male psychology, states that men are expected to be "Success Objects." Of course, for them to be successful, their careers must become the highest priority. And remember, career-focused men must possess strength, competence, and confidence if they are to succeed. Without these traits it is almost impossible for men to become successful or to see themselves as truly "manly." Imagine a male worker going to his boss and asking permission to leave work early because he is feeling "too teary, tender, and vulnerable."

On the other hand, women are traditionally raised to value relationships. A women's self-worth is often strongly tied to the quality of her connections to family and friends. To the extent she feels "connected," she feels good about herself. Few, if any, successes compensate her in the same way as her connections to her loved ones. She might be the mayor or the newly appointed businesswoman of the year, or she may have just won the lottery, but will she consider herself truly successful without being close to family and friends?

Let's show how these differing priorities can be found in an everyday conversation between a husband and wife. In this scene, a husband phones his wife from work, and they have the following conversation:

**Husband:** "Honey, I have to work late again tonight."

**Wife:** "Why, you know I left work early so that we could all go to the kids' open house at school tonight!"

**Husband:** "I know, I'm sorry, but I just can't. I am so far behind, and if I expect to get anywhere, I've got to put in extra hours."

**Wife:** "So what should I tell the kids? You never make time for them."

**Husband:** "Just tell them I had to work and that we'll all do something this weekend. I'll make time, I promise."

Men frequently expend their energies outside the home in pursuit of financial security and career success. While women often pursue these goals, most give greater priority to their relationships and family. These potentially mismatched priorities create problems similar to that between the husband and wife in the previous illustration.

*Ironically, the qualities that allow men to be successful in their work sabotage them in their relationships with women.* Can he be strong, aggressive, and in control at work, and then come home and apply these same qualities in his relationship? If he does, she is likely to see him as dominating and controlling. How can he spend so much time and energy at work and still be his best at home? Interestingly, she may encourage him to be successful in his career even though his success often undermines her relationship with him.

## The Male Mistake

Sooner or later, intimacy does what it is supposed to do—it reveals the man's vulnerable feelings. These feelings are incompatible with his image of strength. What does he do when this happens? Often he tries all the harder to regain a sense of strength and control. Sometimes he throws himself deeper into work, putting in more hours or taking on more responsibilities. Other times he escapes to the garage, the sports channel, or the golf course. In short, he becomes "emotionally divorced" from his partner. He cuts her off emotionally in order to protect his masculine image. *He values himself the most when he is "manly."* He fears that if he is open and vulnerable, he will be viewed as "unmanly" and therefore less attractive. He thinks he will lose her affections. Ironically, he drives her away in his efforts to look appealing to her.

In his attempts to protect his masculine image, he disengages from his feelings. Because of this he is less connected to his emotions, and therefore less intimate with his partner. As a consequence, she is likely to be hurt and angry. Her typical response is to complain about his emotional distance. Curiously, when she expresses her anger, he withdraws even further. What is a man supposed to do?

As a six-year-old child, one of the authors got into a fight with an older boy at school. During the fight the author's parents happened to drive by. At this point, the fighting stopped and he got into his parents' car. He was sobbing and expected comforting from his parents. Instead, his father scolded him and said, "I never want to see you cry again." From that time on, the author confesses that he has found it very difficult to cry and express vulnerable feelings. Again, what is a man supposed to do?

If you are a male reader and you find the male mistake hard to understand, then try this mental exercise. Imagine going to your partner with tears in your eyes and asking for her help. Tell her you are deathly afraid of being beaten up by the guy next door and you need her protection. Picture yourself trying to be convincing. Then, imagine asking her if she finds you attractive. You already know the answer.

## Masked Men

Perhaps the most dramatic images of male strength or "machismo" are those we see on television and in the movies. Many of these action heroes wore masks. Remember the Lone Ranger, Zorro, Batman, and the Green Hornet? They were strong, brave, emotionally non-expressive, and of very few words. They got the job done, but they were hard to know beyond their heroics.

To achieve their purposes, these masked men had to be strong, silent, and focused. Once they'd accomplished their missions they "rode off into the sunset," leaving behind only the image of their strength. The masks they wore protected their identities and also provided a perfect metaphor for how little we knew about the real persons behind the masks. To live up to the masculine ideal of "strength," a man must constantly keep his emotions in check, especially his "weaker" emotions. He must wear an emotional mask.

The real heroes, however, are not the men who ride off into the sunset, but the ones who remain behind and face the challenges of their relationships, especially their intimate ones. They have the courage to take off their emotional masks and be seen for who they really are. This ought to be the masculine ideal. Stay home maskless — don't ride off!

If you are a female reader, does your partner wear a mask? Put differently, how well do you know his emotional side? How does he manage his hurt, fear, and other vulnerable feelings?

## The Emotional Side of Men

Webster's Dictionary defines over four hundred and sixty different human emotions. Socially, however, men are allowed only three: sexual desire, humor, and anger. When men express other emotions, they are at the risk of losing their image of strength. Can you imagine what happens when over four hundred emotions have only three acceptable outlets? This would be like a fire at a theatre where hundreds of people jam a few exits to escape. Some social critics have described men as "emotionally constipated." Without doubt, men overuse or inappropriately express these three emotions.

### Over-Sexed

First, a man is often inappropriate or excessive in his sexual expression. This gets him into trouble. In the extreme, it is the male who is jailed for rape, sexual molestation, and other sex crimes. Even under ordinary circumstances, his sexuality may still be inappropriate. His closeness to his partner may be dominated by sexual feelings. This limits his options. He is compromised in his means of connecting with her. Men often use sex as a substitute for less safe methods of expressing intimacy. Indeed, for many men, sex is the only means by which closeness and intimacy are obtained. For example, after an intense argument with his partner, he often wants to repair the damage by immediately jumping into bed rather than talking about the issues.

### Funny Guy

Sometimes a man's expression of humor can be excessive and inappropriate, especially in the intimate relationship. At the beginning of the relationship, humor is an important part of his repertoire of seduction. It's very effective because it suggests confidence and intelligence. However, in the revealing context of intimacy, inappropriate or overused humor protects him from expressing himself in ways that might make him look weak or unmanly. Humor is used as camouflage for feelings that would leave him vulnerable, weak and out of control. He makes a joke or teases instead of taking a risk to make contact or to express his deeper feelings.

In the short run, making a joke instead of expressing hurt protects him. But when joking is used again and again to protect his vulnerabilities, those closest to him eventually figure him out and sense his weaknesses. In the long run, he is revealed for the very thing he has tried to hide.

## *Mr. Angry*

Lastly, a man's expression of anger can also be inappropriate or excessive. Moderate levels of anger are allowable because of their association with masculine confidence and strength. Unfortunately, weak-appearing emotions such as fear, hurt, and sadness undergo a change and are expressed as anger because of this association. For example, while under attack by his partner, he automatically converts his feelings of hurt into expressions of anger. This preserves his image of strength. If you consider how often hurt can occur in intimacy, this severely impacts the accuracy of his communications.

His anger is hard to understand because it can represent so many other emotions, such as acting angry to mask nervousness or fear. His anger also tends to be either over-controlled or under-controlled. Either way is inappropriate. After trying to maintain control under trying circumstances, many men attempt to minimize the seriousness of the problem by playing it down or even making a joke. When these attempts fail, it is not uncommon for them to explode somewhat violently. Is it any wonder that many wives are confused and upset because their partners are not emotionally available in the relationship?

## The Feminine Perspective

Women have made enormous strides toward equality. Indeed, the feminist movement of the 1960s and beyond has helped lift the shackles of women's second-class status. Feminist writers such as Erica Jong, Betty Friedan, Gloria Steinem, and Germaine Greer have helped create a liberating environment, allowing women access to economic and sexual freedoms.

Some women have liberated themselves better than others. It's a matter of degree. Unfortunately, many women and men stereotype each other in the same old ways. It's precisely these stereotypes that we are forced to deal with. In the following paragraphs we consider the ramifications of not being fully liberated.

## The Feminine Mistake

Intimacy can render a woman invisible. She loses her identity in her efforts to please and care for her male partner. Her script is to play feminine, and this means being nurturing and compliant. This is the role that many women still play. Oddly enough, the better she plays her role, the more invisible she becomes. What does being invisible imply? She finds it hard to make her own decisions. She fails to assert her true feelings. She finds it hard to stand up for herself. She strangles on her own anger and avoids conflict at all costs. As she submits herself to her partner, she loses her identity and privately becomes resentful and bitter.

This is ironic. The harder she tries to be nurturing and compliant, the more resentful and bitter she becomes. The negative feelings must remain hidden, or she is unattractive to herself and her partner. She loses personal control by giving in to him and hiding her true feelings. In this sense, she blames him for being controlling and sees herself as a victim. Actually, the soft, alluring behavior which made it possible for him to look strong and confident has erased her sense of who she is and what she wants. What is a woman supposed to do?

After the initial attraction wears thin, a curious development occurs in a long-term intimate relationship. As she becomes more comfortable with herself and begins to see him in more realistic terms, she starts to assert herself in the relationship. Unfortunately, many men perceive this new development negatively. He may perceive her as attacking his manhood. Is she driving him away, or are they both unrealistic in their expectations?

If you are a female reader and cannot relate to the female mistake, then try this mental exercise. Consider the repercussions of going to your partner and acting bossy, controlling, and demanding. Imagine if you had told him what to do, made him feel like a little boy, and been very convincing about it. Would your partner find you attractive? If this were your dominant personality, would your partner stay with you?

## Damsel in Distress

Television and movies traditionally portray women as sex objects in need of rescue by heroic men. This characterization flies in the face of the hard-fought feminist efforts to elevate women to positions of power and independence. However, as you probably know, the media plays to these stereotypes.

Consider one of the most famous damsel-in-distress stories ever written—*Cinderella*. Cinderella was the downtrodden victim of her abusive stepmother. She was overworked, made to feel unimportant, and saw herself as unattractive. She was totally unable to save herself. She required a prince to rescue her, but not before the fairy godmother made her look beautiful. At the ball, she quickly captured the affections of the prince, who later had to search his kingdom to find her. The rescue is complete when the prince finds Cinderella; the glass slipper fits, and the two live happily ever after.

## Rigid Expectations

Of course, no one seriously argues that this characterization represents reality today. Unfortunately, the media frequently pigeonholes men and women into rigid gender roles, but men and women are far more complicated. Women can perform heroically, often pulling double duty at work and at home. This is especially true of single mothers who often work two to three jobs and raise a family at the same time.

The important point is that rigid sex roles create unnecessary burdens. Women who are portrayed as damsels in distress run the risk of losing their identity and independence. Men who are portrayed as rescuers face the unnecessary burden of having to play strong all the time. Even women who are portrayed as "super-moms" encounter the prospects of early burnout and ultimately raise children who question the role of men in family matters.

## The Emotional Side of Women

Women are still allowed easier access to their emotions, feminism notwithstanding. Often a woman says what she feels when she feels it. This makes her socially adept and in general easier to get along with. She is quicker to talk and make friends. Most people are more comfortable in the company of women. However, this is not always the case. Some women fight like cats and dogs and actually prefer the company of men. In fact, when women are out to lunch with each other, gossip about other women often abounds.

However, a woman's easy access to her emotions can also create problems in her relationships. For one thing, she is so quick to express her feelings about relationship issues that it can be difficult for her to think through her problems. The danger is that she can experience intense emotional reactions. Furthermore, when her emotions go unchecked, the impact may overwhelm her male partner. This creates a gender-based conflict. She blasts her emotions, and he runs for cover. Actually, some women deliberately turn up the volume on their emotions to provoke a response from their otherwise emotionally restricted male partners.

In the early phases of her relationship, she can access a variety of emotions, with the exceptions of anger and sex. Her expressions of anger threaten her femininity. How can she be nurturing and aggressive at the same time? If she allows herself to express anger, then she risks losing him. Tragically, she pays a price for concealing her anger; she loses her identity.

As intimacy develops, her freedom to express anger unfolds. She becomes more secure in the relationship and becomes tired of suppressing her anger for his benefit. On the surface, her new freedom of expression should lead to a healthier relationship. Unfortunately, he may find it difficult to accept her assertions. Instead, he often sees her as aggressive and is threatened by her.

A woman's expression of sexuality often undergoes changes in the course of her relationship as well. While dating, some women view sex as more acceptable within the context of an intimate relationship. This is not true for all women. Some women are liberated from the constraints of old sex role expectations. However, those who are not are less free to initiate sex, expect and demand sexual release, and enjoy sex for its own sake.

The problem at this point is that her partner may resent her apparent sexual disinterest. As the relationship develops, many women become more comfortable with their sexual desires. They feel freer to initiate and enjoy sexual activity. Again, there is a potential problem. Her partner may have difficulty accepting her sexual assertiveness. Some men find this unattractive because it conflicts with their role as the aggressor in the sexual relationship.

Let's pause for a moment and review the key ideas already presented.

## The War of the Sexes

The war between men and women rages on three fronts. First, he wants to be loved for who he is. Who is he? He is a person whose worth is defined by an image of strength. He is supposed to be confident, capable, and in charge of his life. This implies that he is capable of taking care of her—his way. In his efforts to look strong, he stifles his vulnerable feelings, putting himself in an emotional straitjacket.

From her perspective, he is emotionally withdrawn and unavailable. The battle scene is set. He wants her respect and affection.

She wants to make a close personal connection. Neither gets what he or she wants. Both sexes are frustrated. And neither understands the role each plays in the war. He frustrates her need for emotional connection with him. She, in turn, may feel less valued and withholds her affections, including her sexuality. Both feel cheated and blame the other.

The war continues. On the second front, intimacy is lost when she becomes invisible. Her sex role has taught her to be caring and self-sacrificing and to put herself last. She makes sure that everyone else's plate is full. This impacts her partner. Ironically, as she sacrifices herself, he takes her for granted and can even lose respect and interest in her.

While she plays the role of caregiver, she privately keeps score. In other words, she expects a non-negotiated return-in-kind of what she gives. But it doesn't work. First, he assumes everything is fine. If she gives to him, she must love him. Second, her giving to him is not balanced by equal amounts of self-caring and effective negotiation of her needs.

The war rages on. On the third front, intimacy is lost when sex roles change. For example, what happens over the course of a relationship when she begins to strongly assert her needs? For some men, her assertions grow his respect for her. Yet for others, this is a threat to their manhood. Men are supposed to be strong and in control.

From his perspective, if she becomes too strong, he fears he may look weak and unmanly by comparison. From her perspective, she is naturally developing into a mature, assertive woman capable of managing her own needs. In short, her development translates into his loss of power. What's the solution? How do we stop the war?

## The Union of Opposites

Imagine strong and weak co-existing within him. Imagine care for others and self-care co-existing within her. Now imagine a harmony that allows acceptance and equal expression of these opposing traits. This is what we mean by the union of opposites. We are not saying that men need to be more like women or women need to be more like men. Instead, we believe that each gender must integrate the opposing parts within themselves before real intimacy can occur.

Let's see how this can be done by looking at a familiar gender problem. She communicates two opposing points at the same time. On the one hand, she expects him to act strong, work hard, and provide financial security. On the other hand, she needs him to open up emotionally and tell her what's on his mind by sharing his deepest feelings. What's wrong with this picture? Is she sending him double messages? Does she expect him to be strong and weak at the same time?

## His Problem

Let's illustrate this last idea with an example. Mike comes home from work exhausted and with a lot on his mind. Mike's wife, Lauren, who has also had a lousy day at work, nevertheless knows immediately that Mike is upset. Mike is hurting, but he has been taught to look strong and hide his feelings. If he is too open and discloses his feelings to Lauren, he will worry about her judging him as weak, and not measuring up.

Actually, Lauren may or may not be doing this, but in his mind he imagines the worst. She wants him to be strong and manly, and also to be open and share his feelings. Since she hasn't seen him all day, she needs an emotional connection with him. Mike's response is typical of what many men do under similar circumstances. He withdraws, which upsets Lauren.

## His Solution

How does Mike resolve his problem with Lauren? First, Mike must identify, legitimatize, and represent his needs and feelings. This moves him beyond a mere recognition that he is overworked and stressed. Good need management allows him to explore his most fundamental needs and deepest feelings. He can do this through self-examination, or more specifically, need identification.

For example, what really happened at work? Is he angry with someone? Is he frustrated over his work performance? Did someone hurt him? Now, what does he need from Lauren? Notice how these pointed questions help direct Mike's attention to his deepest needs and feelings. Don't expect this to be easy. Men are experts at hiding what they feel. Remember, knowing what we need and feel is critical. We can't manage what we don't know about ourselves.

Next, Mike must redefine what it means to be strong. Strength comes from identifying, legitimatizing, and representing his basic needs and deepest feelings. Underneath Mike's hurt feelings is the need to be accepted for who he is and how well he performs his work. If he stops and thinks about it, he will realize these are perfectly legitimate needs. This new insight will allow him to tolerate his so-called "weak" feelings. For instance, if someone at work hurts Mike, imagine how much courage it would take to express these feelings to Lauren.

*We are endorsing here a nonconventional meaning of male strength.* The usual meaning is to play the "sturdy oak" or be strong and silent. Many men think that the expression of weak feelings makes them unmanly or feminine. We disagree. It takes great courage to identify, legitimatize, and express basic needs and raw emotions, all the while leaving oneself wide open and vulnerable.

Finally, when Mike identifies, legitimatizes, and represents his needs and feelings, he is managing himself well. He becomes someone he can respect in relation to his wife. Effective self-management leads to self-respect. Because Mike respects himself more when he is with Lauren, he also respects Lauren. And in turn, Lauren is likely to respect him also. His positive feelings for her are not dependent on her moods or her ambiguous messages. They are dependent on how well he has managed his own needs and feelings, which are under his control. Mike is self-generating love.

When Mike respects himself, he communicates differently with Lauren. He is vulnerable and strong at the same time. For example, he may say, "I'm hurt," but say it in a way that preserves his self-respect. This can be done when he changes his beliefs about what it means to be strong. He must communicate with an understanding and acceptance that it is courageous to manage his hurt. This is his part of what we mean by the union of opposites.

## Her Problem

A man may also communicate two opposing points at the same time. On the one hand, he expects his partner to be nurturing, compliant, and emotionally supportive. Remember, if she plays this role too well, she runs the risk of losing his love. She also loses her identity and under-respects herself. When overdone, this can be a turn-off to her male partner. On the other hand, he wants her to be strong, independent, and self-respecting. This is exactly what he has been taught to respect in himself. Certainly, in his more confident moments, her strength and independence are a turn-on.

However, in his weaker moments he feels threatened by her independence and assertiveness. He worries he is no longer seen as strong. From her perspective, she is being given conflicting messages. She is expected to be supportive and assertive at the same time. If she is too soft, she runs the risk of losing her identity. If she is too assertive, she runs the risk of being non-feminine, challenging his manhood, and losing his affections.

Let's refer back to our example of Mike and Lauren and flush out Lauren's conflicts. Remember, Mike comes home from work and is very upset. Lauren is immediately aware of his mood and automatically begins to care for him. In fact, this sensitivity is at the heart of her problem. What if Lauren's mood is bottomed out too? Does she nurture Mike at the expense of her own needs and feelings, sapping her own remaining energy levels? If she does, she is under-representing herself. Lauren's caring is then out of balance. She may be afraid that if she nurtures herself, Mike will think she is "selfish" and not caring enough for him. Even if her fears about Mike's reactions are untrue, she could still be critical of herself. In effect, she is saying it is not okay to be self-caring. Too much self-caring is selfish and not feminine.

129

## Her Solution

Lauren must form within herself a union of opposites. She must bring together the opposing parts of herself. Softness must co-exist with assertiveness. Each has its place. She must decide when it's best to use each. This is a delicate emotional balance. Here are some steps she can take.

The first step is to identify her needs and feelings. She must ask herself how she will feel if she caters to her husband. Is she angry at becoming invisible? How does she feel about her partner? Does she blame him for her feelings? Or does she feel uncared for? Fortunately, many women already possess the ability to recognize their needs and feelings. This is an advantage over men. Women are one step ahead.

The next step is to redefine what it means to be caring. She is taught to look after others first and think of herself last. This is out of balance. She is not showing enough self-care. Instead, she must think of caring as a balancing act in which she treats herself as well as she treats others. For every act of other-care, there must be a balance of self-care. By doing this she can avoid resenting her loved ones. However, this will not come easily to her; it will require practice. Many women view self-care as selfishness, a departure from their usual duties.

In short, she must broaden her meaning of caring to include herself. We suggest she study the benefits of balancing self-care with care for others. For example, had Lauren attended to Mike's work stress at the expense of her own needs, she might have resented Mike. And if this pattern continued, she could find herself falling right out of love.

On the other hand, if she balances care for herself with care for Mike, she can maintain respect for herself and safeguard her respect for Mike. For example, when Mike arrives home upset, she could say, "I can't tell who is more stressed, you or me. Why don't you tell me about your troubles and then I'll take my turn." In this way, Lauren balances self-care with respect for Mike. Her needs are under her own control. She is self-generating love.

Finally, when she acknowledges, redefines, and integrates her opposing sides, she becomes someone she respects in relation to her partner. As a result, she respects him. Her positive feelings are under her own control; she is effectively managing her needs. They are not dependent on his reactions or his opposing expectations of her. Even if he does not support her self-caring efforts, she can still respect herself because she has effectively managed who she is in relation to her partner. This not only leads to self-respect, but also greater respect for her mate, and in turn, her mate will show greater respect for her. She is self-generating love.

## Summary

Our gender-based roles give rise to conflicts and form the foundation of the longest war. Specifically, our sex roles restrict us from having a deeper understanding of who we are as relating partners. Conversely, good need management encourages us to reach below the surface of our gender roles to find our most fundamental and common needs. In the process, gender differences are neutralized as we deepen our connections with ourselves and our partners by identifying, legitimatizing, and representing our individual needs. What emerges is a fulfilling union of opposites.

## Personal Exercise

To heighten your sensitivity to gender stereotypes, try the following exercise:

If you are a female reader, answer this question: What bothers me most about men?

If you are a male reader, answer this question: What bothers me most about women?

When we conduct this exercise with a large audience, women typically say things like, men are too obsessed with sex, too egocentric, and emotionally insensitive. Men usually say things like, women are too moody, emotional, and nag too much.

What do these responses have in common? They are all examples of gender stereotyping. We are over-generalizing about the opposite sex. We are assigning traits about women or men based solely on their membership in a gender group. We are ignoring individual differences that certainly exist in each group.

Are your responses similar to ours? If they are, you too are gender stereotyping. The biggest danger is that you respond to your partner as if the stereotype were true. For example, you might blame your boyfriend for being insensitive. Not only is this a stereotype, but you still have the problem of managing your own need to be understood. Stereotyping puts the focus upon our partners' character traits and prevents us from doing the harder work involved in identifying, legitimatizing, and representing our own needs.

# Part III
# Starting Over

# Chapter Seven
# Love Affairs

There are numerous crises in intimate relationships, but few are more threatening and devastating than the extramarital affair. In this chapter, we will explain why affairs occur and how a couple can survive and manage the potential destructive fallout of this kind of betrayal.

## Cheating

Have you ever thought of having sex with someone other than your partner? Even further, have you ever imagined what it would be like to be married to someone else? Most of us have considered these possibilities. In fact, forty to sixty percent of married partners have cheated on their spouses. These percentages vary from study to study and may underestimate the actual numbers. Now, let's bring these statistics to life with a highly infamous example.

Consider one of the most publicized scandals of recent times—the Clinton-Lewinski affair of 1998. Lewinski was accused of being starry-eyed and infatuated by President Clinton's power. However, some people saw her as a victim. Clinton, on the other hand, was accused of abusing his power as President of the United States. Remember the aftermath of this affair? Why did this scandal rock the nation? Why were so many of us obsessed with the sordid details of their sexual affair?

The Clinton-Lewinski affair reminds us of our own vulnerabilities. Some of us can relate to Lewinski's dreamy and unrealistic expectations of love. Some of us can identify with Clinton's use of his position to seduce a young woman without the responsibilities that go along with an intimate relationship. In fact, most of us can relate to the occasional fantasy of someone new.

## Why Do People Cheat?

Why do we betray our partners? There are as many reasons for cheating as there are cheaters. Some of the more common reasons include the excitement and possibility of a new partner, the desire to fall in love again, and the need to escape the conflicts, resentments, and responsibilities of an unsatisfying relationship. However, a closer look at these reasons reveals that what we are really doing is running away from ourselves.

## Escape from the Self

No one knows us better than our intimate partners. They know our strengths and weaknesses. Our partners have the capability to frustrate, hurt, and anger us. They see things about us that we'd rather not face. Ultimately, our partners reveal our flaws, foibles, and imperfections. In short, they reveal the deficiencies in our personalities.

It is the nature of the intimate relationship to illuminate two separate but overlapping aspects of our personalities. First, intimacy makes known the incompleteness of our early emotional development. No other relationship is as powerful in bringing our developmental deficiencies to the forefront. In one form or another, our partners reveal our weaknesses. They see the holes in our personalities. Remember, there is no such thing as perfect parenting. No one escapes childhood without some degree of emotional scarring. Now as adults, our partners bring out these imperfections. They read us like books.

Second, it is also the nature of intimacy to afford relating partners a countless number of opportunities for managing individual needs. Intimacy reveals how well we manage the personal needs we bring to our relationship. How well do we identify, legitimatize, and represent our needs? Or do we withdraw, demand or blame our partners? When we default by choosing the latter set of options, we are not effectively managing our needs. We are running away from ourselves?

Need management is a difficult, complex, and often risky undertaking. For any number of reasons, we pull back from a more active management of our needs. Sometimes we hope our partners will simply know what we need and gratify us. Whatever the reason, chronic poor need management catches up to us, and we begin to pay the price. We become someone we don't like in relation to oru partners.

The temptation is to escape what our partners reveal about us. None of us enjoys having our imperfections thrown in our faces or having to struggle to meet our emotional needs over the long haul of an intimate relationship. We find ways to avoid what intimacy reveals about us. We have affairs, or we are enticed to start over with someone new. The fantasy of a new partner makes love seem easier. We take on a romantic high. We share a romantic pedestal with our new love interest. Everything seems perfect. Love conquers all! However, the excitement of a new love affair is a time bomb waiting to explode. Cheating is not a solution; rather, it is an escape from the self. We are running from what our partners reveal about us. When we run away, we bring the same person, with all of our old problems, into the new relationship. Further, we reinforce running away as a solution rather than facing up to what our partners teach us about ourselves. Unfortunately, the glitter of a new romance is really just an illusion. We can't escape from ourselves.

### A Case Example

Let's showcase these points with an example. Matt and Lisa have been married for eighteen years. For the past five years, Lisa has complained that Matt is emotionally withdrawn from her. In her view, Matt works too much, and when he is at home he spends too much time on the computer. She thinks he is not romantic and does not want to make love to her. Lisa says she has tried everything to make Matt more responsive to her needs, but nothing has worked. Out of desperation, Lisa started an affair in an effort to meet her needs. Now she is racked with guilt and is still frustrated over her loveless marriage.

Is Lisa justified in looking outside her relationship to meet her needs? We don't think so. The bottom line is, Lisa is running away from herself. Let's go over some of the more productive options Lisa could choose.

## Treatment Options

Lisa is at a crossroads in her life. If she chooses to face herself and stay in her relationship with Matt, she will need to do some very difficult things. Our model outlines the steps Lisa will need to take.

### Stop Blaming Our Partners

*Blaming our partners strips us of our power.* Blaming creates the impression that our partners have a hold over us and that we are overly dependent on them to meet our needs. Further, blaming reinforces the outlandish assumption that our partners both create and are somehow responsible for our emotional well-being. In effect, we are saying, "If only you were different, I could be happy." We infer that our love of our partners depends upon how well our partners meet our needs. *Do we love our partners for who they are, or for how well they gratify our needs?*

In Lisa's case, she blames Matt for being emotionally withdrawn and frustrating her romantic desires. This is her excuse for looking outside the marriage to gratify her needs. In our view, Lisa should look within herself for answers. As difficult as it may be, Lisa's problems with Matt actually afford her a unique opportunity for self-growth.

## Analyzing Our Stories

During the romantic phase of our relationships, we describe our partners in very complimentary ways. In short, our depictions of them are very positive, even idealistic. With time, knowledge of our partners naturally broadens as we come to know them more thoroughly. The inevitable conflicts that come with intimacy and the mismanagement of our needs combine to make it easy to tell negative stories about our partners. In brief, we blame them for not meeting our needs.

While our negative depictions of our partners may be perfectly accurate, we are nevertheless spinning our wheels. Remember, it is easier to blame our partners than to manage our needs. Also, remember that we cannot tell explicit stories about our partners without telling implicit stories about ourselves. For example, if we label our partners as controlling, what does this say about us? Are we playing passive roles? If yes, what aren't we doing to manage our needs?

Embedded in our implicit stories are unmet or mismanaged needs. When we mismanage our needs, we don't like the kind of people we are in relation to our partners. We are actually falling *out* of love with them. Also, we have unwittingly set ourselves up to blame our partners. This is exactly what Lisa has done. She blames Matt for being emotionally withdrawn and uses this explicit story to justify her love affair. Remember, Lisa is racked with guilt. Her poor need management has lowered her esteem for both herself and Matt. She does not like the kind of person she has become in relation to Matt. She is falling out of love with him.

## Managing Our Needs

Effective need management consists of three overlapping but important steps—need identification, need legitimization, and need representation.

## Need Identification

First, we must identify our needs. We can't manage what we don't know about ourselves. Also, knowing what we need is how we begin to define who we are in relation to our partners. A good parent accurately identifies her or his child's needs and by so doing instills within the child a respectable sense of identity.

In Lisa's case, she needs to specifically identify what she needs from Matt. She can do this by asking herself what she feels strongest about. Obviously, Lisa wants romance with Matt. This is her need.

Now, she must legitimatize and manage her need. Lisa should accept the appropriateness of her need. This will strengthen her resolve to represent it to Matt.

Next, Lisa must express her need to Matt in a way that balances respect for Matt with respect for herself. To begin, she might ask for a moment of Mart's time. As artificial and overly formal as this may seem, it sets a conversational agenda that is respectful of Mart's time. Lisa could further convey her respect for Matt by trying to anticipate the possible impact her need might have on him.

Throughout this process, Lisa should express the deepest feelings associated with her need. This important step deepens Lisa's connection to herself and paves the way for greater intimacy with Matt. *Lisa can be no more intimate with Matt than she is with herself.*

For example, Lisa could describe how happy she would feel if she could have a romantic connection with Matt. She might also convey her deepest fear that Matt will reject her. To lessen her fear, Lisa could make a positive reference to a prior romantic interlude she and Matt have shared. But perhaps most difficult of all, Lisa must make the gratification of her need for romance secondary to how well she manages her need. This means that Lisa places self and partner esteem and the quality of her relationship above her immediate need for romance. And this is the critical point: Lisa must make a switch in her thinking.

## Shifting Our Thinking

At this point, Lisa needs to shift her thinking in a new direction. She needs to think in terms of what she can do to create romance with Matt by how she manages herself. This gives Lisa more control and is an important part of what we mean by self-generating love. As much as we may like or dislike our partners' qualities, it is more important that we like the kind of people we are in relation to our partners.

In the long run, how we manage the needs we bring to our partners is more important to us and the health of our relationships than the gratification of our needs. This takes us to our next point that effective self-management promotes respect for ourselves and our partners at the same time.

## Magical Changes

Now, here's the magic. When *we* manage our needs well, we are self-generating love. We grow esteem for ourselves and our partners. We have become the kind of people we like in relation to our partners. As a result, our partners love us more. In other words, as we manage our needs in a respectful way, we get matching amounts of love and respect back from our partners. In the Lisa example, if she were to manage her need for romance in a way that would respect both herself and Matt, she could expect greater love from Matt.

There's still more magic. As Lisa manages her needs well, she actually elevates the probability of gratifying her needs. Partners who respect one another are more likely to meet each other's needs.

# Personal Exercise

If you or your partner has had an affair, consider what this means from the perspective of the model. In other words, do a need management evaluation on how well you managed your needs prior to your affair. To do this, imagine you're in a classroom being graded on how well you have managed your needs. What would your report card look like? Give yourself a letter grade, *A* through *F*, after answering the following questions:

- How well were you able to identify your needs?
- If you could identify your needs, did you legitimatize them?
- Did you try to balance respect for your partner while managing your need(s)?
- Did you make the gratification of your needs more important than the health of your relationship?
- Did you evaluate the success of the management of your needs by whether they were gratified or not?

Let's assume the worst. Your report card shows a *D* or *F* grade. This explains why you had the affair. Need management with your partner was too difficult, so you looked outside your relationship for an easy solution. Now let's further assume you have come clean with your partner and she or he has forgiven you. Now what do you do?

Go back to the time just before your affair and put into practice the principles of effective need management. Just the process of doing this is a refreshing rewrite of your past personal history. Notice that for the first time you are putting the health of the relationship above your personal needs. It's actually not too late to reclaim the esteem you lost for yourself and your partner.

# Chapter Eight
# Separation, Divorce, and Starting Over

There is no pain that compares to the hurt we feel when we lose someone we love. Most of us endure physical injury better than the deep emotional wounds of separation and loss. In fact, death of a spouse, divorce, and domestic violence top the list of psychological stressors. These injuries can and often do *affect* us so profoundly that some of us choose never to love again. Those of us who do start over often find the task intimidating and extremely difficult. The good news is that when we've healed from the devastations of a lost love, we are much more prepared for our new love relationships.

## Terminating Relationships: The Right Reasons

From time to time, our clients ask, "Are there any justifiable reasons for ending a relationship?" Based on what we've said so far, you might conclude the answer is no. But there are valid reasons for ending a relationship. Unfortunately, some relationships are toxic and need to be dissolved.

Domestic violence is grounds for separation and divorce. This does not mean there is absolutely no hope for this type of problem. However, the abused partner needs to separate and be protected in a safe environment. The abuser must willingly and actively seek psychological treatment. In fact, it is advisable that both partners enter therapy. At some point in the future, if the abused party agrees and is confident of the abuser's rehabilitation, there is a chance for the relationship to recover.

The exploitation of children is another reason for legitimately terminating a relationship. Any form of physical, sexual, or emotional abuse obligates the non-offending partner to take quick, decisive, and effective action to ensure the protection and safety of children. This of course could include the options of separation and divorce. There can be no question about treatment being mandatory for the offending parent. And every precaution must be taken to safeguard the future safety of the children, especially where reunification with the rehabilitated parent is a consideration.

## The Wrong Reasons

Many people end their relationships prematurely and for the wrong reasons. In Chapter Seven, we discussed the novel idea that cheating partners were really running away from themselves. Cheating partners are guilty of poor need management and invent justifications for their affairs. As we've previously stated, it is possible to repair a relationship damaged by betrayal, assuming both partners are willing to commit to rehabilitating their relationship.

Many divorcing couples are in violation of the conventional marital vow, "For better or for worse." When things such as individual differences, unresolved conflict, disease, or physical debilitation interfere with personal need gratification, some partners assume there is justification for ending the relationship. In effect, they believe their partners exist solely for the purpose of gratifying their needs.

This is a common marital trap because most, if not all, of our personal needs are indeed legitimate. We therefore make the understandable assumption that our needs should be gratified, sometimes at any cost. However, when personal and immediate need gratification becomes a higher priority than effective need management, then the health and preservation of the relationship is at peril.

But when our highest priority is effective need management, then partners like who they are in relation to each other. This, in turn, translates into increased understanding and mutual respect. By prioritizing need management, we place the health of the relationship above the immediate gratification of our individual needs. And there is an added bonus. Couples who respect one another are more likely to gratify each other's needs.

Another common but faulty reason for terminating a relationship is chronic unresolved relationship conflicts, especially where children are involved. All too often, couples throw in the towel when faced with long-standing, unsettled arguments. Do you have ongoing fights over money, sex, family, kids, or religion? If these disputes remain unresolved, how do you feel about yourself and your partner? Are the disputes a breeding ground for divorce?

Prolonged couple conflict is an example of one or both partners not effectively managing their needs. Personal need gratification becomes more important than the health of the relationship. Whatever the issues, the troubled couple is entrapped by poor need management and is in danger of relationship failure. The solution is not to pull the plug, but to learn the skills of effective need management.

## Poor Need Management

Poor need management is like a highly contagious virus. A cold or flu virus normally incubates within four to ten days and we get sick. But "emotional viruses" incubate much faster, sometimes in a nanosecond. In other words, when our partners mismanage their needs, we feel it instantly. Feelings of frustration, hurt, and anger are ignited.

For example, an overworked spouse reacts loudly and negatively to her husband when she discovers the kitchen sink full of his dirty dishes. He reacts with equal sharpness, claiming he had a hard day at work and wants to relax. She feels slighted for his indifference to her workload. He feels disrespected both for how he was spoken to and for being unappreciated for putting in a long day at the office. She mismanaged her need for a clean kitchen sink, and he mismanaged his needs to be acknowledged for his efforts and to be spoken to in a considerate manner.

The mismanagement of her needs provoked the mismanagement of his needs. Need mismanagement compromises the immediate health of the relationship. Had the overworked wife asked for a moment of her husband's time, identified, legitimized, and gone on to represent her needs, the fight never would have occurred. Similarly, if the husband had effectively managed his needs, the argument could have been avoided or, in the least, minimized.

## Common Denominator

*Chronic need mismanagement is the most common reason for wrongfully ending a relationship.* For a variety of reasons, partners find it difficult to effectively represent their individual needs. Fear of rejection, conflict, loss of approval, embarrassment, or other intimacy deficiencies undercut effective need management. Instead, partners argue and fight, give up prematurely and unnecessarily on their partners, and often look outside their relationship for answers, including affairs. All of this, of course, weakens the long-term health of the relationship.

# After the Breakup—Single and Alone

You're all alone now. What are you going to do? Should you remain single and avoid the hardships and perils of intimate life? Or should you jump back into the turbulent waters? If you should decide to rejoin the ranks of the bold and committed, we have some recommendations.

## Managing the Emotional Fallout

Remember the sad wash of feelings that swept over you after your last breakup? Did you experience loneliness, guilt, anger, depression, or maybe a sense of failure? If you did, don't be alarmed. This is quite typical. *However, before you can successfully start a new relationship, you must learn the origin of these feelings and how to effectively manage them.* Turning our backs on the past is an open invitation to repeat the same or similar emotional difficulties in future relationships.

Underlying these difficult emotions are perfectly legitimate needs that have been thwarted, frustrated, or otherwise mismanaged. Imagine that you've just been physically injured. Would you simply wipe away the blood? Or would you examine the nature of the wound? Is it an abrasion, a laceration, or a deep puncture? In other words, to treat the wound appropriately requires knowing the type of injury. Similarly, the difficult emotions following a breakup inform us as to the type of relationship problems we've suffered. Just like a physical injury must be examined before it can be appropriately treated, we must evaluate our painful emotions for what they tell us about ourselves, specifically, our capacity for intimacy.

Our most painful emotions are like road signs that map out the deeper parts of who we are, our fundamental needs. When these basic needs are poorly managed, the result is toxic feelings. For instance, when Lauren divorced Brent after ten years of marriage, she had accumulated a mountain of frustration, hurt, and anger. She justified her breakup by blaming Brent for being "emotionally constipated." By her accounts, Brent was cold, distancing, and emotionally unavailable. Actually, her difficult feelings were the result of poorly managed needs.

## Examining Your Previous Relationship

Who was at fault? It's easy to point an accusatory finger at our partners or even ourselves. But this is counterproductive. *Your partner should not be the one in control of how you feel.* Instead, we advocate self-examination and effective need management. In this way, you are not telling a negative story about your partner or yourself. What you are doing is taking responsibility for the love that you did or did not generate for your previous partner. Ask yourself, to what degree was your love self-generated?

## Positive Stories

Remember when your romance was hot? You were awestruck with your partner's exciting qualities. She or he was perfect. Recall how you used to describe your partner to your friends and family. All of the stories were glowing. You were in love. However, it was character-based love. You fell in love with your partner's character traits.

## Negative Stories

What happened? Your positive stories morphed over time. After countless face-offs with your partner, the friction of interpersonal differences took its toll. Poor need management set the stage for negative storytelling, which over time began to outweigh the positive stories.

In Brent and Lauren's case, she originally saw him as mellow, unassuming, and well-focused. Over time, intimacy does what it always does: it reveals us—all of our faults, foibles, and imperfections. Lauren began to see Brent more completely and realistically. Her perceptions of his qualities changed. Unfortunately, she began to see him as distancing and withdrawn.

Why did this happen? Lauren's love was character-based. Initially, she saw Brent as possessing traits that would make her happy.

Because of these traits, she expected him to gratify her needs. Of course, Lauren's needs were ultimately her own responsibility. Brent had his own needs to manage. When Lauren's needs were not gratified, she began to tell negative stories about Brent.

For instance, when Brent was preoccupied, she saw him as withdrawing from her. Her view of Brent changed not because Brent was essentially different, but because she did not effectively manage her needs. She expected Brent to do it for her. *The ultimate responsibility lies with Lauren, not Brent.* Remember, it is easier to tell a story about your partner than it is to identify, legitimatize, and represent your own needs.

# Starting Over and Reconnecting

Starting over with someone new first requires that we reconnect with ourselves. This involves identifying the needs that we did not effectively manage in our previous relationship. The focus is entirely on ourselves and not on our partners. A complete self-analysis will help us evaluate how well we managed our needs in our previous relationships. In the process, it may be helpful to study the stories we told about our partners, especially the negative ones. Remember, these stories contain information about our mismanaged needs.

As we've said, we can be no more intimate with our partners than we are intimate with ourselves. To be intimate with ourselves requires that we know what our needs are and that we develop the skills for managing them. Therefore, taking an inventory of our needs and how well we managed them is crucial.

## Need Management Inventory

What needs were not effectively managed? What impact did this have on you and your partner? Now, see if you can identify which ones they were. How might you have more effectively managed them? What might have been different in your relationship?

After close self-examination, Lauren discovered that near the end of her relationship with Brent, she despised him because he didn't meet her need for intimate personal talk. Lauren discovered that her story about Brent as being emotionally constipated revealed the importance of her need for intimate talk.

## Starting a New Relationship

Imagine that you had an infinite amount of time and an inexhaustible supply of money with which to search for an ideal mate. Where would you begin your search? And what qualities would you look for in a potential partner?

The work of partner selection is daunting, so we often look to any and all sources for answers. Many people turn to dating and matchmaking services. All of these services emphasize partner compatibility. Searching for compatibility is one way to answer the question of how to start over. But it's character-based and therefore flawed and limited.

The social psychological research supports the notion that similarity breeds liking. In other words, there is some truth to the expression that birds of a feather flock together. But there is much more to the story. If this were not the case, would the divorce rate hover at over fifty percent? Should you base the next phase of your life on the flip of a coin? We don't think you should.

Similarity leads to liking, but this is not the same thing as partner compatibility. You can like someone, but not get along with him or her. Partners may share similarities, but not be compatible. And yet other partners may be dissimilar and still be compatible. You get the point: compatibility is overrated.

## The Myth of Compatibility

The illusions of compatibility are seductive during the beginning of our relationships when we least know our partners. This is when it is easiest to make our partners anything we need them to be. During romance, positive stories flourish. But what happens over time?

The pursuit of partner compatibility is understandable, but ultimately limited. For example, who would not want a partner with similar qualities to our own? Unfortunately, what we are initially attracted to is prone to change, and for numerous reasons. Positive stories become negative ones. Compatibility alters over time with our changing moods and perceptions. What we once fell in love with, we now may hold in contempt and scorn.

Partner compatibility and character-based love are virtual bedfellows. In both cases, the source of our love lies outside ourselves. When a partner is initially perceived to have compatible characteristics, it is often assumed the business of relating will flow almost effortlessly. Sadly, this is a fallacy.

Additionally, traits once viewed as positive may later foster negative stories about our partners. Compatibilities convert to irreconcilable differences. These inevitable changes impact the quality of our love. When character-based love holds sway, our love rests on the shifting ground of our perceptions. The person *we think* we love becomes more important than *how* we love. In this sense, we are dependent on our partners' qualities rather than self-generating love.

Making matters worse, we frequently confuse compatibility with convenience. Are you familiar with the expression "geographically desirable"? Potential partners take on a measure of desirability which is based solely on how convenient they are to date. Mate selection is then pursued within a range of travel which is not overly burdensome on our time and financial resources. Admittedly, we find our lifelong partners in convenient ways. They work with us, attend the same school, go to the same church, or know the people we know. Are our partners really compatible, or merely convenient? And even if they are perceived to be compatible, we don't think it's enough.

Again, consider this possibility: You have an infinite amount of time and an inexhaustible amount of money with which to search for an ideal partner. Where would you begin such a search, and what traits would you look for? Unknowingly, we answer these challenging questions by selecting partners we believe we are compatible with, because of convenience, or simply because we think we are "in love." But there is another way to think about it.

## Beyond Compatibility: Who vs. How

Obviously, partner compatibility has some value. And dating services emphasizing compatibility can be useful in finding an intimate partner. But again, they are not the complete answer. The character of one's partner is important, but how we generate love for this person is even more critical. In other words, we advocate the *how* of loving over the *who* of loving. *How* we love preserves the passion for *who* we love. In the long term, the how is more important than the who because the who is always changing. The who brings us together; the how holds us together.

For example, consider the marriage of the late president Ronald Reagan and his wife, Nancy. Imagine Nancy falling in character-based love with Ronald. She would be attracted to his rugged good looks, his driving ambition, and his endless energy and charm. Now, remember how admiring we were of Nancy because she remained devoted to Ronald even though Alzheimer's disease had radically altered his character? In our view, her love was self-generated. The how of her love prevailed over the who of her love.

## Self-Generated Love

The love we feel for our partners ought to be under our own control. Love should not be seen as coming solely from our partners' character traits. Instead, we advocate self-generated love. We generate love by how effectively we manage ourselves. Strengthening our skills of need identification, need legitimatization, and need representation improves long-term intimacy. We are now no longer dependent on our partners' qualities, behaviors, or moods. Love becomes our own creation. Good self-management is the best and most reliable source of love.

Consider again Ronald and Nancy Reagan. In Ronald's later years, the ravages of Alzheimer's disease erased his good looks, intellectual abilities, and driving ambition. His memory and coherence had diminished; he wasn't the same person. In spite of this, Nancy's love and devotion remained steadfast. Her continued care of Ronald suggests that her love was self-generated. It was under her control and was not dependent on Ronald's eroding character traits.

# Using the Model for Starting Over

Self-generated love can be used even at the beginning of a new relationship. Keep in mind, the *how* is always more important than the *who*. What does this mean in the context of dating? Imagine you've just found an encouraging prospect. Your search has led you to someone you think is compatible, and all the signs of romantic love are in place. The initial groundwork has been laid. Character-based love has served its purpose. What's next?

The same principles that apply to long-term intimate relationships apply to dating. You must effectively manage your needs. Remember the three pillars of self-management: need identification, need legitimization, and need representation. What needs might be present at the start of a relationship? For most of us, the list probably includes things like fun, romance, and getting to know the prospective partner. With this in mind, let's look at an exciting young couple in love.

### A Case Example
Yvette and Derrick have fallen madly in love with each other. On the surface, they seem compatible, and both are looking at the possibility of a long-term relationship. Like most people in the early phases of dating, Yvette wants to have a little fun and romance while getting to know Derrick. Her needs are perfectly legitimate. Now, how does she manage them?

Yvette can manage her needs by expressing specifically what she means by fun and romance while at the same time considering Derrick's interests. As simple as this may seem, think about what's happening. By expressing her needs, Yvette has defined herself a little better and in the process taken on greater self-respect. Her consideration of Derrick's interests shows him respect. She is balancing respect for herself and Derrick.

Next, Yvette can make need management even more effective by expressing the deepest feelings associated with her needs. For instance, if dancing fills Yvette with fun, excitement, and closeness, she should find an appropriate way to share these feelings with Derrick. This way she connects with herself, and this will increase the likelihood of a better connection with Derrick.

She should also anticipate what Derrick might expect romantically. By doing this, Yvette is going beyond the immediate gratification of her needs and is considering what is best for her newly developing relationship with Derrick. Yvette must keep in mind that her success at need management should be evaluated by reference to what she does, not by how Derrick initially responds to her. By following these steps of good need management, Yvette can grow esteem for herself as well as Derrick.

### Attracted to Whom?

The model also gives us a deeper understanding of why we are attracted to some people and not others. Most commonly, we explain our attraction to others by reference to their qualities. Of course, this is character-based love. In contrast, self-generated love teaches us that the love and respect we create for our partners results from the love and respect we generate for ourselves. Self-respect, in turn, comes from effective need management. Self-respecting people tend to attract partners who will show them similar respect. Simply, we attract a good partner by learning to more effectively manage our needs.

## Personal Exercise

Do you have a history of attracting the wrong type of partner? Or have you ever thought about why your partners always seem to change over time? If you answered yes to either of these questions, we recommend that you take a *need management inventory* to assess your capacity for self-generated love.

## Need Management Inventory

The following questions are designed to assess your capacity for effective need management. At the end of each section you can rate your skills for the three levels of need management—need identification, need legitimization, and need representation. Give yourself a 1 for *poor*, a 2 for *fair*, a 3 for *good*, and a 4 for *excellent*. Then add your score for each category and refer to the "Rungs of Need Management" scale to get an overall assessment of your personal need management skills. Higher scores will put you nearest to or in Rung 1, which is where each of us ought to be as effective need managers. Lower scores will put you on Rung 2 or Rung 3, indicating that your need management skills need tuning up.

### Need Identification

How well do you identify your needs? Note that some of your needs will be easier to identify than others. And some will be very difficult to pinpoint. Also, keep in mind our feelings and needs often overlap; they both point out each other. Frequently, more than one need can be activated at the same time, complicating the task of need identification.

**Overall my need identification skills are**

poor _____

fair _____

good _____

excellent _____

### Need Legitimization

How well do you accept your needs? Do you see your needs as strengths or weaknesses? Are your needs important? How much do you worry about how your partner views your needs?

### Overall my need legitimization skills are

poor _____

fair _____

good _____

excellent _____

## Need Representation: Balance of Self and Other Respect

When managing your needs, do you over-respect yourself? Do you over-respect your partner? How well do you balance respect for yourself with respect for your partner?

### My skill at balancing self and other respect is

poor _____

fair _____

good _____

excellent _____

## Expression of Need and Feeling

How well do you express your needs and the deepest feelings associated with them?

### My skills of need and feeling expression are

poor _____

fair _____

good _____

excellent _____

## Prioritizing of Needs

To what degree do you prioritize effective need management and the quality of your relationship above the immediate gratification of your needs?

### My skills of need prioritization are

poor _____

fair _____

good _____

excellent _____

## Evaluation: Self vs. Partner

When managing your needs, how well do you focus on what you are doing as opposed to focusing on your partner's responses?

**My skills at evaluating myself are**

poor _____

fair _____

good _____

excellent _____

These are not easy questions to answer. Hopefully, you have learned a little more about your need management skills. Now take a look at three broad categories for assessing your ability to manage your needs and the feelings associated with them. See where your score puts you.

**Rung 1** (Scores in the 20-24 range) Your need management skills are excellent. You do very well at balancing self and partner respect. You effectively express your needs and the deepest feelings associated with them. You prioritize need management over immediate need gratification. You evaluate your success by reference to what you do and not your partner's responses.

**Rung 2** (Scores in the 16-18 range) Your need management skills are characterized by the use of coaxing, power, confrontation, persuasion, and manipulation. Your primary problems center around over-respect for yourself and reduced respect for your partner. You tend to pursue need gratification over the health of your relationship.

**Rung 3** (Scores of 8 and below) You typically under-manage or don't manage your needs at all. Your patterns of self and partner relating are characterized by withdrawal, over-compliance and submission. Fundamentally speaking, fear is your worst enemy.

As a result, the typical negative feelings you have for yourself and your partner are contempt, resentment, and diminished respect.

Using this need management inventory, you can assess your capacity for effective need management, whether you are currently in an intimate relationship, are just starting one, or have just ended a relationship.

How much would you pay for a healthy intimate relationship? What is the value of your self-respect? What is the value of your partner's respect for you? Achieving Rung 1 success is not easy, but it pays off in huge emotional dividends.

\* \* \*

Mastering Rung 1 means we are self-generating love. In other words, we are effectively managing our needs. Love is under our control. The health of the relationship is the highest priority. Our intimate relationships are in a league of their own. They are incomparable. The intimate relationship, in spite of its difficulties and challenges, makes possible the greatest fulfillment and personal growth. It is the new womb of development.

It is our hope that the need management ideas and tools contained in this book will help you to create, or strengthen, your intimacy skills, and help you to enjoy and sustain the inherent fulfillments of your intimate relationship.

# Glossary of Key Terms

**Character-Based Love**—A type of love in which a person's attraction to another person is based upon the other person's personality traits or qualities.

**Emotional Brain**—The part of the brain that develops early and organizes our feelings and early relationship experiences.

**Formative Relationship**—The first relationship, usually with our parents, which helps develop our personalities and exerts a strong influence over the course of our lives.

**Gender**—An identification of whether you are born and raised male or female.

**Infant Love**—The earliest attachment bond between a mother and her infant.

**Intimacy**—The degree of closeness between two people.

**Model**—An organized viewpoint that gives understanding and direction to our experience.

**Need**—A desire, want, or wish that pushes or pulls us toward a goal.

**Need Gratification**—The fulfillment of a desire, want, or wish.

**Need Management**—The effective handling of a desire, want, or wish in an intimate relationship.

**Rational Brain**—The higher part of the brain which processes information in logical and complex ways.

**Revealed Relationship**—A feature of the current intimate relationship in which the less developed aspects of our personalities are made known.

**Romantic Love**—A type of character-based love experienced as passionate and compelling. It is what we usually mean by "falling in love."

**Self-Generated Love**—The creation of love for ourselves and our partners in the context of the intimate relationship which occurs as the result of the effective management of our needs.

**Sex Role Stereotypes**—The assumption of traits or expectations about males or females.

**Storytelling**—Blaming or labeling our partners for failing to gratify our needs.

# References

Boszormenyi-Nagy, Ivan, and Barbara R. Krasner. 1986. *Between Give and Take: A Clinical Guide to Contextual Therapy.* New York: Brunner/Mazel Publishers.

Bowlby, John. 1980. Attachment and Loss: Vol. 3. Loss: Sadness and Depression. New York: Basic Books.

Elliot, T.S. 1956. *T.S. Eliot's Poetry and Plays: A Study in Sources and Meaning.* Chicago: The University of Chicago Press.

Farrell, Warren. 1986. *Why Men Are the Way They Are.* New York: McGraw-Hill.

Goleman, Daniel. 1995. *Emotional Intelligence: Why It Can Matter More Than I.Q.* New York: Bantam Books.

Gottman, J.M., & Levenson, R.W., 1985. *Physiological and Affective Predictors of Change in Relationship Satisfaction.* Journal of Personality and Social Psychology 49(1): 85–94.

Jourard, Sidney M. 1971. *Self-Disclosure: An Experimental Analysis of the Transparent Self.* New York: Wiley-Interscience.

Keen, Sam. 1983. *The Passionate Life: Stages of Loving.* San Francisco: Harper and Row.

Rubin, Zick. 1973. *Liking and Loving: An Invitation to Social Psychology.* New York: Holt, Rinehart & Winston.

Shakespeare, William. 1599-1601. *Hamlet: The Tragical Historie of Hamlet, Prince of Denmark.* Act I, Scene iii.

Sternberg, Robert. 1986. *Triangle Theory of Love.* Psychology Review 93:119–135.

Tannen, Deborah. 1990. *You Just Don't Understand.* New York: William Morrow and Co.

Wile, Daniel. 1988. *After the Honeymoon: How Conflict Can Improve Your Relationship.* New York: John Wiley & Sons, Inc.